FOUNDATIONS OF MODERN PSYCHOLOGY SERIES

Richard S. Lazarus, *Editor*

E D W A R D J. M U R R A Y

Associate Professor of Psychology and Director of the Clinical Psychology Training Program, Syracuse University; Diplomate in Clinical Psychology; researcher and author of numerous articles on many areas of motivation and emotion, including hunger, pain, fear, conflict, sleep, sex, dependence, affection, and independence.

Motivation
and Emotion

PRENTICE-HALL, INC., *Englewood Cliffs, New Jersey*

CMenSP

TO MY WIFE, LOUISA, AND MY DAUGHTERS,

SUSAN, MARTHA, AND SARAH

MOTIVATION AND EMOTION, *Edward J. Murray*

PRENTICE-HALL FOUNDATIONS

OF MODERN PSYCHOLOGY SERIES

Richard S. Lazarus, *Editor*

PRENTICE-HALL INTERNATIONAL, INC., *London*
PRENTICE-HALL OF AUSTRALIA, PTY., LTD., *Sydney*
PRENTICE-HALL OF CANADA, LTD., *Toronto*
PRENTICE-HALL OF INDIA PRIVATE LIMITED, *New Delhi*
PRENTICE-HALL OF JAPAN, INC., *Tokyo*
PRENTICE-HALL DE MEXICO, S. A., *Mexico City*

Designed by Harry Rinehart

C–60397(p), C–60398(c)

Foundations
of Modern Psychology
Series

The tremendous growth and vitality of psychology and its increasing fusion with the social and biological sciences demand a new approach to teaching at the introductory level. The basic course, geared as it usually is to a single text that tries to skim everything—that sacrifices depth for superficial breadth —is no longer adequate. Psychology has become too diverse for any one man, or a few men, to write about with complete authority. The alternative, a book that ignores many essential areas in order to present more comprehensively and effectively a particular aspect or view of psychology, is also insufficient. For in this solution, many key areas are simply not communicated to the student at all.

The Foundations of Modern Psychology is a new and different approach to the introductory course. The instructor is offered a series of short volumes, each a self-contained book on the special issues, methods, and content of a basic topic by a noted authority who is actively contributing to that particular field. And taken together, the volumes cover the full scope of psychological thought, research, and application.

The result is a series that offers the advantage of tremendous flexibility and scope. The teacher can choose the subjects he wants to emphasize and present them in the order he desires. And without necessarily sacrificing breadth, he can provide the student with a much fuller treatment of individual areas at the introductory level than is normally possible. If he does not have time to include all the volumes in his course, he can recommend the omitted ones as outside reading, thus covering the full range of psychological topics.

Psychologists are becoming increasingly aware of the importance of reaching the introductory student with high-quality, well-written, and stimulating material, material that highlights the continuing and exciting search for new knowledge. The Foundations of Modern Psychology Series is our attempt to place in the hands of instructors the best textbook tools for this purpose.

Preface

The area of motivation and emotion is a controversial one. There is some question whether this is one area or two. There are some psychologists who would eliminate motivation and emotion entirely as a topic for general psychology. They regard the subject as the last refuge of the humanists, the vitalists, and the teleologists. Perhaps they are right, in a way, because it is when we consider motives that the analogy between man and machine breaks down. Science, however, is not restricted to simple analogies; the area of motivation and emotion forces us to consider the true complexity of man as a biosocial organism.

The field of motivation and emotion is so disorganized that it is very tempting to take one of several simplifying courses. First, a writer can embrace one of the competing monolithic systems—learning, psychoanalytic, field, or hedonic theory. Second, it is possible to restrict one's view to a single source of information—animal experiments, human experiments, clinical observation, or anthropological field studies. The final simplification is to consider only physiological drives or only psychodynamic variables or only social forces. I have found that all of these simplifying strategies result in serious distortions.

The approach in this book is pluralistic and integrative. I have not presented the material from a single theoretical viewpoint because I like the clash of ideas and because I do not think that a really adequate theoretical framework for human behavior has been developed yet. I would prefer that the student remain a little confused than to straight-jacket his mind. I have tried to communicate the excitement of behavioral science by emphasizing the birth, decline, and rejuvenation of concepts, the theoretical significance of the newer discoveries, and the never-ending struggle for understanding. At the same time, I have tried to integrate the laboratory, field, and clinical studies, trying to show how these are all valid and complementary sources of knowledge. Finally, although it is not possible to present an exhaustive survey in a book of this length, I have attempted to give examples from the entire spectrum of motivation and emotion—hunger, sex, fear, curiosity, affection, and achievement.

Edward J. Murray

Contents

Contents

Contents

ix

Conceptions
of Motivation

The human being is a marvelous organism capable of perceiving events, making complex judgments, recalling information, solving problems, and putting a plan into action. Yet this intricate apparatus can be used for a variety of ends—to plan for war as well as to explore outer space, to humiliate another person as well as to comfort the sick, to achieve recognition, dominance or friendship. The uses to which a person puts his human capabilities depends on his motivation— his desires, wishes, wants, needs, yearnings, hungers, loves, hates, and fears. Perhaps an example will make this clearer. Suppose we imagine three young men in college.

I

1

They have identical intelligence and scholastic aptitude. Yet one of them is getting straight A's, the second C's, and the last is failing. Differences in motivation may account for these differences in performance.

The first young man comes from a poor immigrant family. His parents have set their hopes on his becoming a successful professional man. They encouraged and rewarded him for high grades from early childhood, so he developed a very powerful desire to achieve and is not afraid to work hard. Actually, he sets high standards for himself and feels satisfied only with an A.

On the other hand, the second fellow comes from a wealthy family. He has no worries about the future. After college he will join his father's business. He is not motivated to get high grades. In fact, he may view the first young man as a grind, perhaps somewhat boorish. He, himself, aims only for the gentlemen's C.

The explanation of the failure is probably more complicated. However, a case of a father and son I saw recently illustrates the kind of situation that could account for it. The father had come from a poor family but had pulled himself up by his bootstraps and was now a successful, hard-driving lawyer. He expected his son to do as much. The son, however, was frightened of the father and convinced he could not do as well. He tensed up on exams; his heart pounded and his hands sweat. His anxiety interfered with his performance and he began to fail.

In the first case, the student was motivated to get high grades. The second student was not. The third student was motivated towards achievement, but a competing emotional motive prevented his success. In all cases, the processes of perception, memory, and thinking were adequate for the task, but actual performance depended on the motives and emotions.

An interest in motivation is not limited to psychologists. We all have our private ideas about what makes people tick, and, in fact, some such conception may be necessary for getting along in life. We frequently ask what a person wants, what may influence him, what is important to him. A successful salesman learns when to appeal to economy and when to status needs. A doctor who forgets that patients need a little sympathy, as well as medicine, may find his practice dwindling.

Motivational concepts are woven into many of our social institutions. The punishment for killing another human being depends on the killer's motivation and whether the killing was done coldly or in the heat of emotion. A politician who introduces a bill for legalized gambling declares that man has an instinct for gambling so that it can never be eradicated. In dealing with international tensions our statesmen may make many motivational assumptions—for example, that war is inevitable because man has a destructive instinct, or that people will invariably select freedom if given the choice. These assumptions may or may not be correct.

For centuries philosophers and theologians have been debating the nature of man. In doing so, frequently, they have been asking questions and drawing conclusions about motivation. For example, the fifteenth-century English philosopher Thomas Hobbes believed that man is basically selfish, destructive, and brutish. From this he concluded that, in order to prevent chaos, it is necessary for individual men to submit to the power of an absolute monarch. In the next century, John Locke, a strong advocate of parliamentary government, wrote that the original nature of man is peaceful, with feelings of good will and cooperation towards his fellows.

It is clear, then, that our conceptions of human motivation have pervasive influences on our lives. The question is, how accurate are these conceptions? Both Hobbes and Locke argued convincingly for their positions, although one suspects that their political convictions dictated their views on human nature. Which one is right? For many, the answer is a matter of conviction, or personal experience, or the logic and force of the argument, or majority vote. But these are not the ways of science.

The method of science is to formulate clear theoretical hypotheses and test them by carefully controlled observation. The scientific study of human motivation and emotion has begun relatively recently. In this book we shall describe some of the methods and results of psychologists who have studied motivation scientifically. Isolated facts are of little interest, though, unless they are integrated into some over-all theoretical conception. The field is so new that there is no single generally accepted theoretical framework for motivation. Instead, there are a number of competing conceptions inherited from philosophy or borrowed from biology. We shall describe these major conceptions now and refer to them throughout the book.

COGNITIVE THEORIES

The oldest view about man is that he is essentially a rational being. He has conscious desires and uses his capacities to fulfill them. This was the basic idea of ancient philosophers such as Plato and Aristotle, of medieval philosophers like St. Thomas Aquinas, and of the more recent thinkers including Descartes, Hobbes, and Spinoza. It is also the opinion of the average man on the street. A person thinks of what he wants and tries to figure out ways of getting it.

The notion of man's *will* played a large role in these theories. Will was held to be one of the "faculties" of the mind on a par with thinking and feeling. Since an individual can control his will, he is responsible for his actions. Man is not buffeted about by forces over which he has no control; he can shape the world to fulfill his desires. For Epicurus the issue was so vital for the future of man that he attributed freedom to the atoms of physical matter so that man could also be viewed as free.

Psychologists have not found the concept of will—free or otherwise—to be very useful in explaining why a person has particular desires and wants. The search has headed in the direction of finding the sources of motives in man's biological heritage and his experiences in social living. For a person may not even be aware of the motives that are influencing his behavior. Therefore, motives are usually distinguished from thinking and other cognitive processes.

Nevertheless, a few psychologists today do vigorously maintain an essentially cognitive approach to the problems of motivation. Perhaps the best example is George A. Kelly, who has little use for the term motivation. Rather than view behavior as something that has to be put into motion, he believes that behavior is continuously active, the main problem being the selection of alternatives. The decision a man makes depends on his personal constructs—his ideas, values, and attitudes about the world. Thus, in many backward countries of the world, the personal constructs are such that a decision is made between exploitative capitalism and communism. As Kelly sees it, a different set of personal constructs could result in a decision between authoritarianism and democracy in the broadest sense.

The typical reaction of many psychologists to such a cognitive theory is that, although it presents a fine analysis of the decision process, the motivational variables remain hidden. Underlying the choice between one political system and another are the desires of the people for food, security, and self-esteem. The personal constructs of a person certainly determine the routes over which these goals are sought, but the cognitive analysis is not incompatible with the idea that there are basic motives the person is trying to fulfill.

HEDONISTIC THEORIES

Interwoven with the philosophizing about man's reason and will was a second idea—that man seeks pleasure and avoids pain. This idea, which is called hedonism, is an attempt to explain why people behave as they do, and it should not be confused with hedonism as an ethical system in which a person purposely builds his life around pleasure-seeking and pain-avoidance. The hedonistic or hedonic theory of motivation can be traced back to the ancient philosophers, but it was most prominent in the eighteenth and nineteenth centuries.

Hedonism was rejected by psychologists along with most of the other rationalistic theories of philosophy. Psychologists have not been too happy with the dependence of hedonistic theory on a private knowledge of a person's experiences. What do we know about another person's inner sensation of pleasure? One man's meat is another man's poison. Another reason for rejection is that hedonism tends to become circular: A man is said to seek pleasure; if he seeks something, then, it must be pleasurable. But what about a man who seems to seek failure? Or what about suicide? There are also people who appear to reject pleasure-seeking as a way of life. The Puritans, for example, avoided pleasure as a sinful thing. Of course, you could say that the Puritans obtained pleasure from abstention, but with this sort of argument one can explain behavior only after the fact, and hedonism loses all predictive power.

Nevertheless, in recent years hedonism has had something of a renaissance. Psychologists such as Paul T. Young and David C. McClelland have suggested sophisticated versions of the hedonic theory. Instead of relying on subjective reports of pleasure and pain, however, these scientists use objective measures of approach and avoidance behavior. They are developing an experimental hedonism. As we shall discuss later on, there is now considerable evidence for innate physiological mechanisms for pleasure and pain.

McClelland's hedonic theory uses an affective-arousal model. What this means is that certain environmental stimuli innately arouse a state of pleasure or pain, with a corresponding tendency to approach or avoid such stimuli as goals. The degree of pleasurable or painful affect (or emotion) aroused depends on a person's prior adaptation. For example, a loud sound might be disturbing to an individual under normal circumstances but not after several hours at a jet airport. Small discrepancies from an adaptational level are pleasurable but larger ones aversive. This helps explain why a person sometimes gets pleasure from the tickle of a very gentle electric current but pulls away when it is increased.

Motivation, for McClelland, consists in the learned anticipations or expectations of a goal as arousing positive or negative emotional reactions. Goals previously known to arouse pleasure are approached, those that produce pain are avoided. In this sense, McClelland defines all motives as learned. The affective arousal is innate but the anticipation is acquired. Thus, it appears, the venerable concept of hedonism can be developed as a useful scientific theory.

INSTINCT THEORIES

The real beginning of scientific theories of motivation came with Charles Darwin's theory of evolution. Darwin thought that certain "intelligent" actions are inherited. The simplest of these are the reflexes, such as the sucking reflex of the young. Others are more complex, such as the tendency of birds to avoid man without prior experience with him. These more complex actions were called instincts, an idea which can also be traced back to antiquity. Darwin believed instincts arise through natural selection. Instincts are usually thought of as being more flexible than reflexes, and so permitting more variable behavior.

Around the turn of the century, theorists like William James, Sigmund Freud, and William McDougall developed the instinct doctrine as an important explanatory concept in psychology. Some writers thought of instincts as somewhat mechanical and blind, but the most systematic theorist, McDougall, thought of them as purposive, inherited, goal-seeking tendencies. He wrote, "We may then define an instinct as an inherited or innate psycho-physical disposition which determines its possessor to perceive, or pay attention to, objects of a certain class, to experience an emotional excitement of a particular quality upon perceiving such an object, and to act in regard to it in a particular manner, or at least, to experience an impulse to such an action." *

Obviously, many discrete actions in various species could be classified as instinctive. But the goal of science is to simplify, so the aim was to find a limited number of basic instincts that could account for all behavior. Some theorists put a good deal of weight on one or two instincts, like Freud's emphasis on sexual and aggressive instincts. McDougall was more typical in assuming a handful. In 1908 McDougall's list was: flight, repulsion, curiosity, pugnacity, self-abasement, self-assertion, parental, reproductive, hunger, gregariousness, acquisitiveness, and constructiveness.

The instinct doctrine held sway in psychology for the first quarter of this century but then began to run into difficulty. First of all, there was a disturbing tendency for the list of instincts to grow. Each author added a few more

* W. McDougall, *An introduction to social psychology.* New York: Barnes and Noble, 1960 (Original, 1908).

until by the nineteen-twenties the list totaled nearly 6,000 instincts, including an "instinct to avoid eating apples in one's own orchard." In the twenties, John Watson and other members of the behaviorist school of thought, along with many cultural anthropologists, began an attack on the instinct theory, striving to explain as much behavior as possible on the basis of learning, even talking about a "psychology without heredity."

Although instinct theory has appeared to be dying a slow death, it has never been entirely abandoned and recently has been revived by the European ethologists such as Nikolaas Tinbergen and the American comparative psychologists such as Frank Beach. These scientists stress detailed descriptions of instinctive behavior, particularly in lower organisms. Thus, they have moved from armchair theorizing about instincts to laboratory experiments. Their work also relates instinctive behavior to underlying physiological mechanisms.

An example of this new study of instincts is the discovery of the phenomenon of imprinting. You may have observed a mother duck swimming in a park lagoon with a string of baby ducks following behind. This is an instinctive pattern in fowl and birds but it develops only under special circumstances. There is a critical period for a few days after hatching from the egg when a baby duck becomes attached to any one of a great variety of stimulus objects. Ordinarily, this is the mother duck, but the duckling may also become attached to a hen, a boat, or a quacking human being. You may recall, in this connection, the story of the ugly duckling. Once the attachment is made, however, the object for following becomes imprinted and irreversible. The ugly duckling, in fact, would never return to its beautiful mother swan.

DRIVE THEORIES

The most prominent concept in the motivation field today is that of *drive*. This concept was introduced by Robert S. Woodworth in 1918 to describe the "energy" that impels an organism to action as opposed to the habits that steer behavior in one direction or another. Although Woodworth meant the term to refer to the general supply of energy, people soon began to talk not of "drive" but of several different "drives," such as hunger, sex, thirst, and so forth. They meant tendencies toward or away from specific goals. Thus, in many ways the idea of drives resembles that of instincts. Nevertheless, drive theory has been much more acceptable to most psychologists.

One reason for this preference is that drives have been introduced one by one on the basis of careful experiments and given specific operational definitions. An operational definition of a drive is a specification of both the conditions under which the drive can be said to be functioning and the means of measuring it. Thus, a drive may be measured by the hours of deprivation of food, the concentration of sexual hormones in the blood, or the intensity of an electric shock. The reduction of a drive can be defined by operations such as the satiating of hunger with food, sexual exhaustion, or the termination of shock.

The logic of drive theory was greatly advanced by the concept of homeostasis introduced by the physiologist Walter B. Cannon in 1932. According to this concept, a state of disequilibrium is set up in the body whenever the internal conditions deviate from a normal steady state. Psychological drives are one way the body attempts to return to equilibrium. Thus, when the nutritional supply is depleted in the body, the hunger drive is activated, food is sought and consumed, and so equilibrium is restored. Thus, motivation came to be defined as the drives arising out of homeostatic imbalance or tension.

The homeostatic drive concept has had its greatest influence in the field of learning. For example, in 1943 the learning theorist Clark L. Hull assumed that all behavior is motivated by homeostatic drives or secondary drives based upon them. Internal drive states are thus set up by depriving an animal of food, water, or sexual experience. These drive states reflect homeostatic imbalance, or internal tensions.

Hull also assumed that all *rewards* are ultimately based on the reduction of a primary, homeostatic drive. A reward of food reduces the homeostatic imbalance produced by hunger. A human being or a laboratory animal will learn a response to get a reward. Secondary rewards, such as social approval, are effective because they have been associated with food and other primary rewards in the past.

A considerable amount of interest, recently, has centered around external sources of motivation, as opposed to the inner, homeostatic determinants. For example, a goal object itself, in addition to functioning as a reward for learning, may also serve to arouse motivation. A man may not feel particularly hungry until he smells the delicious aroma of a chicken frying on the stove. The smell, sight, or taste of the food is said to operate as an incentive. In social situations, particularly, the motivating effect of the goal is often much more apparent than that of internal factors. Motivation is aroused by incentive pay, by the sight of a pretty girl, by a television commercial.

Although drive theory, in one form or another, still stands as the cornerstone of modern thinking about motivation, it has been found increasingly wanting by many psychologists. The controversy has centered around three major questions: Are primary drives synonymous with internal physiological need? Are all incentives and rewards based on homeostatic tension and tension-reduction? Are all social motives based on the primary physiological drives such as hunger, sex, and pain? These questions and others will be considered in the following chapters.

A DEFINITION OF MOTIVATION

It is clear that different theorists have different conceptions about motivation. Nevertheless, there is general agreement that a motive is an internal factor that arouses, directs, and integrates a person's behavior. It is not observed directly but inferred from his behavior or simply assumed to exist in order to explain his behavior. Motivation is distinguished from other factors that also influence behavior, such as the past experience of the person, his physical capabilities, and the environmental situation in which he finds himself, although these other factors may influence motivation.

A motive is usually broken down into two important components. First, the term *drive* refers to the internal process that goads a person into action. Drive may be influenced by the external environment—by the temperature, for example—but the drive itself is internal. Second, a motive is terminated by reaching a *goal* or obtaining a *reward*. The goal or reward is assumed to have some reducing or satiating effect on the internal goad, so that after reaching a goal or being rewarded sufficiently, the motive no longer directs behavior for some period of time. A goal or reward may involve an external object such as food, but the drive-terminating process itself is internal.

Some psychologists add that motivation also includes a *conscious desire* for something. This is sometimes called a *want*. A desire or want is related to the goal-selecting function of motives. Other psychologists, however, believe that a desire or want is too subjective to be of value scientifically. They would simply take a person's verbal report of his inner feelings as one aspect of behavior that is influenced by the inferred motive.

Motivation
and Behavior

At any given time a person is motivated by a variety of internal and external factors. The strength of each motive and the pattern of motives influence the way we see the world, the things we think about, and the actions in which we engage. Imagine a student walking down the street exposed to all sorts of sights and sounds. He cannot pay attention to all these stimuli, so he responds to only certain ones. Unusual stimuli may arouse his curiosity—he stops to watch a building being demolished. Curiosity may not be the only motive; if he has had a particularly trying day he may tarry to enjoy the destructiveness involved. He may have

9

2

fleeting thoughts of similar destructiveness towards his professor, girl friend, or society in general.

Eventually, when he resumes his walk, he may notice a restaurant and realize he is hungry. He may muse over the fact that he had passed this restaurant many times before and never realized it was there—he had not been hungry on those occasions. As he orders his meal he finds himself flirting with the waitress. He enjoys it, but she is tired and has a headache so she views him as a bore. Still, since she wants a tip, she gamely kids along with him.

Later as he studies in his room he concentrates on learning his math or biology or language. As he gets tired he pushes himself on with thoughts about the grades he will need to get into a professional school. He may pause to think about his parents and wonder if they appreciate how hard he has to work to become the success they want. Asleep at last, he may have a confused dream in which his professor—looking suspiciously like his father—shakes his head sadly as he hands back an examination paper, the waitress from the restaurant leers at him, and he operates a crane knocking down academic-looking buildings.

In this example, we can see the operation of the motives of curiosity, aggression, hunger, sex, fatigue, pain, achievement, and affection on perceiving, thinking, acting, talking, learning, and dreaming. The motives fluctuate and arrange themselves in various patterns at different times. Some of a person's motives are always operating, and his behavior is largely controlled by them. These effects can be demonstrated in laboratory experiments that afford careful control over the motives and provide objective measures of the behavior. Let us examine the ways psychologists have studied the effects of motivation on various psychological functions.

THE MEASUREMENT OF MOTIVATION

How do we know when a person is motivated and by what particular motive? How do we measure a motive? There are two general ways of doing this—measuring certain external conditions that are thought to produce a drive and measuring certain aspects of the behavior of the person, which reflect his motives.

The use of external drive conditions to measure motivation is most applicable in the laboratory. There, for example, hunger is usually measured by the *number of hours* during which a subject has been *deprived* of food. Hunger may also be measured by the percentage of body weight lost, by the number of calories consumed in a period of time, and by other procedures. Pain is frequently measured by the *strength of electric shock* administered to a laboratory animal. An achievement drive may be aroused by *instructions* which suggest that a particular task is a measure of intelligence. In general, *deprivation, stimulation,* and *verbal instructions* are the main means of experimentally arousing a drive.

However, these drive-establishing conditions are not the same as a drive. Very often they do produce a drive but not always. When a person goes completely without food for several days he does not feel hungry. Instructions about a task may arouse achievement in some people but not others. There has to be some effect on behavior before we can say that a drive-producing condition has actually produced a drive.

One of the chief effects of a drive on behavior is to influence the selection of goals. If a laboratory animal turns his nose up at food but drinks water, we say he is thirsty but not hungry. So, too, some people may respond to instructions appealing to achievement and others to friendship; we say, then, that the former are motivated by achievement, the latter by affiliation. Rewards also depend on motivation. An animal may learn to run through an alley to get to a receptive female but not for food. A gold star is an effective reward for some children but not others. In general, the existence of a motive is inferred from the goals a person selects and the rewards that are effective.

Motivation is also inferred from other aspects of behavior. The vigor, frequency, and speed of a response is sometimes an indication of motivation. The dominance of a theme in a person's conversations, fantasies, and dreams also suggests certain underlying motives. A person who talks and thinks of nothing but making money might be said to be strongly motivated in this direction. Inferring motivation from behavior, however, is difficult and, at times, misleading. This is because behavior is determined not only by motivation, but also by the present situation and past experience. Thus, a man may have learned that having money is a means of gaining recognition. For him, the motive is really for recognition; getting money is just a means to this end. So, too, a man may gain recognition in one situation by talking about money and in another by talking about cultural activities. It is only when we know a person's past experience and can control the situation in which he finds himself that we can accurately infer motivation from his behavior. In the following sections we shall give examples of how motivation is related to various kinds of behavior in which the influence of the present situation and past experience is controlled.

LEARNING AND PERFORMANCE

The effect of motivation on learning and performance has been a matter of central importance to psychologists for a number of years. A number of issues fundamental to all kinds of behavior have been stated and explored in this context. Because of the widespread implications of the problem, the experimenters have attempted to purify the process by using very simple animals— white rats usually—learning very simple responses. The idea is that the basic nature of the effect of motivation on learning and performance can be more easily understood in this simplified situation and then generalized to more complex behavior.

A basic question is whether increasing a drive leads to an increase in the goal responses appropriate for that drive. Does increasing hunger increase eating? Does increased copulation follow an increase in the sexual drive? This relationship has, in fact, been demonstrated for a number of drives.

Since goal responses come very close to being reflexive, however, it would be very surprising, indeed, to find that they did not vary with drive level. A question of greater theoretical significance is whether increasing a drive facilitates the learning of a *new* response to get the appropriate reward. In other words, will a motivated student learn more than an unmotivated one? A large number of experimental studies with animals, children, and adults has shown that all kinds of maze-running, bar-pressing, and verbal responses will be learned faster when drive is increased to moderate levels. Furthermore, after the response has been well learned, its performance depends on the degree of drive.

Does motivation always facilitate learning and performance? A considerable amount of evidence now suggests that increasing a drive up to a certain point facilitates behavior, but extreme degrees of drive may actually result in a deterioration. This effect may be due to physical weakening, the emergence of irrelevant and interfering responses, or the induction of an emotional state.

The exact point at which a drive begins to interfere with learning and performance depends on the nature of the task. Very simple tasks are facilitated by the strongest drives any experimenter has used, although when drive level reaches an animal's point of physiological exhaustion even simple tasks would be expected to deteriorate. As tasks become more difficult, the facilitating level of drive gets lower and lower. This relationship was formulated some years ago by two comparative psychologists and is known as the Yerkes-Dodson Law. It may be simply stated in the following way: The optimum motivation for learning decreases with increasing task difficulty.

The validity of this law has been demonstrated a number of times. One of the more recent and clearest studies was done by the English psychologist P. L. Broadhurst. He trained rats to swim through an underwater maze shaped like the letter Y. At the fork, the rat had to choose between a brightly lit door leading out of the water and a dark door which remained locked. This discrimination choice could be made very easy by having the correct door very bright, and thus quite different from the incorrect door, or difficult by having the doors closer in illumination level. Broadhurst used three levels of task-difficulty—easy, moderate, and difficult.

Motivation consisted of the need for air after being under water. Groups of rats were kept submerged for 0, 2, 4, or 8 seconds before being permitted to swim through the maze. Thus, there were four levels of motivation and three levels of task difficulty. The measure of learning was the number of correct choices made at the fork of the Y maze.

The results are shown in Figure 1 where it can be seen that the optimum level of motivation varied with the difficulty of the task. With the easy task, motivation was optimum at 4 seconds of air deprivation, with only a slight fall-off thereafter. The optimum deprivation for the difficult discrimination was 2 seconds, with a very drastic decline beyond that.

Somewhat comparable results have been found with college students doing tasks similar to examinations. A moderate degree of tension or anxiety may help, but an overanxious student may not be able to learn and perform as well as his ability would suggest. Furthermore, in line with the Yerkes-Dodson Law, anxious subjects do well on easy tasks but their performance deteriorates on difficult ones. In general then, motivation facilitates learning and performance only up to a point, the exact point depending on the nature of the task.

So far, we have been discussing the drive side of the motivational process. The reward side, however, is equally important. Of course, the number of times

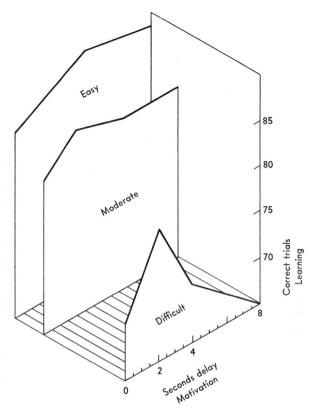

Figure 1. A three-dimensional model illustrating the Yerkes-Dodson Law. Rats were deprived of air by restraining them under water for a varying number of seconds and were then permitted to escape by selecting the correct door. Optimum motivation for learning depended on the difficulty of the choice task. (After P. L. Broadhurst. Emotionality and the Yerkes-Dodson Law. J. exp. Psychol., 1957, 54, 345–352.)

an organism is rewarded for making a response determines the strength of that response-habit. Reward, then, is primarily a problem in learning, not motivation. Nevertheless, the nature of a reward appears to have a direct effect on motivation by making a goal more or less attractive. This effect is sometimes called the incentive value of a reward.

It has been demonstrated, for example, that if an animal is given several hundred food pellets every time he runs down a runway he will run faster than if he is given only a dozen or so. Similarly, the taste of food is important. An animal will press a bar more frequently for a food mixture containing saccharine than for a plain one. On the other hand, he will press less frequently if citric acid has been added. These aspects of reward have a direct effect on motivation just as the value or prestige of a prize has a direct effect on the interest of a person in working to get it.

PERCEPTION AND ATTENTION

The perception of the external world—through the senses of seeing, hearing, smelling, tasting, and so forth—depends to a large extent on the nature of the physical stimulus presented. Nevertheless, other factors also influence both the selective perception of a particular stimulus out of those impinging on an individual at any given time and the way the stimulus is interpreted. Factors such as past experience—whether the person is set for, or anticipating, certain stimuli—and motivation are involved.

The role of motivation in attending and perceiving has been demonstrated in a large number of experiments. For example, moderate hunger (or thirst) tends to increase the number of food- or water-related items seen by subjects in ambiguous pictures. An extreme example is the thirsty man in the desert who begins to see mirages of cool, refreshing, palm-shaded lagoons. So, too, complex social motives like achievement and cultural values may influence perception. But the effects are often complicated and difficult to study. Thus, although moderate hunger facilitates the perception of food-related items, extreme hunger may have the reverse effect, possibly because we tend to avoid seeing what we cannot have. In addition, many early studies did not take the operation of the *expectations*, or *set*, of the subject into account. The instructions given to a subject might *set* him to anticipate or not anticipate items related to his motivation. Because of these problems, there is still a great deal of debate about the exact influence of motivation on perception.

In one of the best-controlled studies in this area, J. C. Gilchrist and L. S. Nesberg have presented very convincing evidence for the effect of motivation on perception. They asked college students to refrain from eating for a period of 20 hours. They then asked the students to make perceptual judgments just after eating lunch, just after the time they would have eaten dinner, and just after they would have eaten breakfast the next morning. The perceptual test consisted of matching the brightness of colored slides containing pictures of a T-bone steak, fried chicken, and so forth. Each slide was presented first at a standard brightness, and the students were asked to study it. Then, after a few seconds, the slide was presented again, at either a higher or lower level of brightness, and the students were required to turn a knob to adjust the brightness to match that of the earlier presentation. Although the students believed they were making accurate judgments, there was a systematic error: As they got hungrier, they made the pictures of food brighter and brighter. Control subjects, who had not gone without food, did not show this progressive change. The authors also showed that thirsty students made pictures of ice water, orange juice, and other liquids brighter as they got thirstier.

Finally, Gilchrist and Nesberg demonstrated that these results were not due to an effect of motivation on vision in general, but limited to perceptions related to the motive. One thirsty group was asked to adjust the illumination of neutral pictures (such as mountains, trees), as well as those of ice water and orange juice. The results showed that the illumination levels of the thirst-relevant objects were set at increasingly higher levels than those of the neutral scenes. Furthermore, when the subjects were given a drink of water, there was a dramatic drop in the brightness adjustment of the thirst-relevant pictures and only a minor drop in the adjustment of the others.

Fear and other negative motives may also have an effect on perception. Some evidence suggests that certain individuals use a *perceptual defense* with emotionally disturbing stimuli, especially those personalities who tend to avoid unpleasantness. There is some question whether such people literally do not perceive the disturbing stimuli or whether they fail to report them, or even think about them, because of anxiety or embarrassment.

Fear may also lead to a misinterpretation or distortion of perception. Thus, a group of playful Puerto Rican teenagers may seem menacing to an apprehensive Irish cop. When fear is great enough, the perception may be so distorted as to be called a hallucination—as with a mental patient who sees threatening shapes in the darkness. This sort of phenomenon was demonstrated some years ago by Henry A. Murray. At a house party for his daughter's friends, Murray asked five eleven-year-old girls to rate a number of photographs cut from magazines on a nine-point scale of maliciousness. That evening he conducted for them a game called "murder," in which the lights were turned out and one player stalked the others. The effect was greater than Murray had anticipated—that night one girl had a nightmare and several others refused to sleep in her bedroom. Anyway, after the game of murder, Murray asked the girls to rate the photographs again and found a dramatic increase in the ratings of maliciousness.

REMEMBERING AND FORGETTING

Motivation also affects memory. For example, if a person is asked to look at photographs of faces and later describe them, he will remember them in line with his feelings and attitudes at the time he saw them and at the time he is trying to remember them. Because of this tendency, a great deal of the eye-witness testimony given in courtrooms tends to be inaccurate and distorted. Psychologists have performed a number of studies in which a still picture or a movie of a crime is shown to people just once, as would be true in witnessing a real crime. Details are forgotten, nonexistent weapons remembered, and the actions of one person attributed to another.

There is a general tendency for people to remember pleasant events more than unpleasant ones and to retain facts that fit in with their already existing ideas rather than those that challenge them. But this does not always hold. We all recall unpleasant events if they are vivid enough. An important factor seems to be whether remembering an incident causes a person discomfort at the present time.

An experiment demonstrating a particularly forceful type of memory distortion, called repression, was performed by A. F. Zeller. He attempted to show that an experience of failure threatening the self-confidence of a person could interfere with the retention of material learned just before the failure experience. First, he asked college students to memorize a list of nonsense syllables. He would give a meaningless syllable such as MOV and the students would learn to respond with something like BIV. After they had learned their list perfectly, they were asked to perform a cube-tapping task in which a cube held in the hand must tap out a pattern on four cubes on the desk. Here is where failure was induced: No matter how well they did, the subjects were told that they had failed and that no one with such a poor memory could ever hope to get through college.

After this experience, the students were asked to run through the list of nonsense syllables. This time, it was found that their memory for this material was adversely affected even though failure had not been directly associated with the nonsense syllables. Moreover, the interference with memory for nonsense syllables continued over a period of three days, although it had been previously demonstrated that students could retain the material that long under normal circumstances. Control subjects who had not experienced any failure with the cubes had no difficulty.

When the threat to self-confidence was removed, memory returned. The students were asked to return and perform the cube-tapping test in easy stages with success assured. They visibly brightened up after this and when tested for their memory of nonsense syllables, they did as well as they had at the beginning.

Thus, it can be seen that motivation and emotion affect how and what we remember and forget. If we couple this influence with the effect of motivation on perception, it becomes clear that the information we have at any given time is highly selected by our personal motives and attitudes. Think about this the next time you are having a political debate. For example, a physician and a man with elderly dependents may be talking about the same bill for medical care for the aged but may perceive the issue quite differently and retain quite different information about it.

THINKING AND FANTASY

As we have seen, motivation is important in determining what information a person perceives and retains. Motivation also plays a role in how he uses information in the symbolic processes of problem-solving, creative thinking, dreaming, and the everyday flow of thought. These processes are internal, of course, and, therefore, not directly observable. We are all familiar with them through introspection, but introspective reports may be easily distorted and unreliable. Therefore, psychologists have tried to devise situations in which the operation of these symbolic processes is reflected in more readily measured objective behavior. These include experimental situations, problem-solving tests, and written fantasies.

We can think of symbolic processes as ranging in degree of organization from the solving of a rigidly structured problem through more loosely constructed creative work to the almost total formlessness of daydreaming or, better yet, nightdreaming. It may seem logical to think that more organized thought is motivated while the free-flowing forms lack motivation. Yet one of the important contributions of psychoanalysis has been to point out the motivational pattern in seemingly meaningless bits of behavior such as dreams, slips of the tongue, jokes, and the rambling free association of the psychotherapy patient. Sometimes the motivation is obscure, sometimes a person is unaware of it, but it is likely that motivation is an important determinant of the entirety of integrated, idle, and bizarre thoughts experienced by an individual.

To begin with, motivation is important in the solving of structured problems. Problem-solving is differentiated from the acquisition of simple habits in that an interrelationship between the parts of a problem must be understood for a solution. It may be thought of as the assembling of discrete habits in a unique way to fit the requirements of a situation. This is sometimes said to be the highest form of human thought—it is involved in the work of scientists, inventors, engineers, business innovators, and government planners.

Beginning with the pioneering studies of Wolfgang Köhler, some of the best experiments on problem-solving have been done with chimpanzees. The thought processes of these highly intelligent animals are more similar to man's than are those of most other animals, and they can be studied under controlled laboratory conditions. The role of motivation in the problem-solving of chimpanzees was investigated by Herbert G. Birch in the apparatus shown in Figure 2. The animals were given a series of problems that required the use of strings and sticks to pull in an orange slice placed outside a cage. Since the animals were taught to use the strings and sticks separately, the problem was not to acquire a simple skill but to combine skills to get the reward.

Birch varied motivation by depriving the animals of food for 2, 6, 12, 24, 36, and 48 hours at different times. The different levels of drive had quite interesting effects on the problem-solving. At the lower levels, the animals took longer and showed fewer insightful solutions. They were easily diverted and frequently played with the sticks and strings. At moderate levels of drive—especially around 24 hours of deprivation—they were efficient and purposeful. They were directed towards the food but flexible in using their skills to get it.

One of the most interesting results was that, beyond the optimum 24-hour deprivation period, the chimpanzees became increasingly inefficient. This result is consistent with the Yerkes-Dodson Law described earlier in this chapter. Apparently, the animals were so hungry that they focused on the food to the exclusion of the other relevant objects. They reached out for the food or thrashed about with the short stick. As they failed they screamed and threw temper tantrums. They did no better than when weakly motivated, but for totally different reasons.

Creative fantasy is another form of thinking that may be influenced by motivation. In fact, it has long been thought that a person's fantasy may more accurately reflect his motives than direct questioning. For example, if

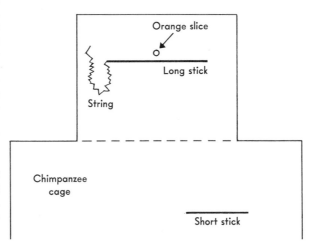

Figure 2. Diagram of a problem given to chimpanzees. A chimp can't reach the food with the short stick nor can he reach the long stick. The solution is to pull in the string with the short stick, then pull in the long stick by the string, and finally use the long stick to get the food. (After H. G. Birch. The role of motivational factors in insightful problem-solving. J. comp. Psychol., 1945, 38, 295–317.)

you ask a person his hopes and fears he may censor his account because he knows that some of them are unrealistic and that some of them are not socially approved. These inhibitory factors are not as strong in the make-believe world. Therefore, as clinical psychologists have found, an otherwise uncommunicative child will reveal a great deal about himself, if he can act out his fantasies with dolls or puppets. So, too, adults disclose their hopes and fears in writing stories about pictures or responding to ambiguous inkblots. The same principle is used in literary analysis, where an understanding of the personality of a great author is sought in his creative writing.

SOCIAL AND EMOTIONAL BEHAVIOR

A motive may also have widespread effects on the general social and emotional behavior of an individual, if it is powerful enough. During World War II, an experiment at the University of Minnesota by Ancel Keys and his associates explored the effects of prolonged semi-starvation; the purpose was to plan for the rehabilitation of famine-stricken areas. Conscientious-objector volunteers subsisted on a greatly reduced food intake for a six-month period, with marked weight loss and physical weakness resulting. Psychologically, they became preoccupied with thoughts of food and lost interest in their usual intellectual activities, girl friends, and social gatherings. Sustained concentration became difficult. They became moody, apprehensive, depressed, and apathetic. Sparkle and humor were absent from their conversation. Most striking to the men themselves was the deterioration in their social and moral standards—they licked their plates, were rude to visitors, and sometimes were unable to resist the temptation to cheat on their diets.

The authors point out how much the behavior of the men was dominated by the always-present hunger. In the past, famine has given rise to migration, crime, and revolution. In the Minnesota study, the subjects became very apathetic about democratic processes. So, too, the starving people of backward areas will have little concern about either democratic or totalitarian ideologies until their most pressing needs are met. It is well to remember this when we deal with poorly nourished populations in Asia, Africa, and Latin America.

Fear and anxiety may have even greater effects on social living. We need only think of how we live today under the constant threat of nuclear annihilation to see some of these effects. We enter into an ever-spiralling arms race that seems to increase tension rather than reduce it. We frantically entertain extreme solutions like preventive war or pacifistic surrender. We distort the meaning of every slight movement of the enemy and he ours. We grow suspicious and distrustful of one another. Most of all we deny the danger but remain uneasy in our daily existence.

CONFLICTING MOTIVES

With all that has been said, it should not be assumed that motives always affect behavior in a simple and direct manner. Several motives may be operating simultaneously, and the responses required to satisfy them may be incompatible. This conflict was shown in a classic experiment by Neal E. Miller. He trained hungry rats to go down a runway to get food from a cup. Thus, they learned to *approach* the goal. Later, the animals were shocked at the food cup, setting up a tendency to *avoid* the goal. Since approaching and avoiding a goal are incompatible, a conflict was established. The animals went part way down the alley and alternated between approach and avoidance.

An experiment that illustrates this kind of approach-avoidance conflict with human beings was done by Russell A. Clark. He attempted to show that experimentally induced sexual motivation would have the same effect on fantasy as has been shown for drives like hunger. Male college students were asked to write stories about neutral pictures flashed on a screen after they had been shown a series of slides of life-size nude females. Contrary to expectation, the stories of these students contained significantly fewer sexual themes than those of a control group not shown the nude slides. Apparently, what happened was that the students were embarrassed or made to feel guilty, with the result that sexual themes were blocked out, or inhibited.

In order to test this possibility, a second experiment was done in a situation noted for reducing inhibitions—a fraternity beer party. After an hour or so of alcohol consumption, the group was shown the nude slides and subsequently asked to write stories about the neutral pictures. This time the stories contained more sexual themes than a control group at another fraternity beer party not shown the nude slides. In fact, both alcohol groups showed more sexual themes than the groups in the first experiment.

In these studies, there were at least two motives operating—sex and guilt. Most people feel too guilty about sexual matters to express them openly. Specifically arousing sexual motivation may only serve to increase the guilt. However, drinking alcohol is a dependable method of reducing inhibitions and feelings of guilt. Under these conditions the inhibited sexual motive can emerge and influence our thoughts and behavior.

Finally, a word should be said about unconscious motives. In the Clark study, just described, the students may have had some private thoughts of a sexual nature that they were too embarrassed to write down. Sometimes, however, guilt or some other inhibiting motive is so great that not even thoughts about the underlying motive can be permitted to emerge. The motive becomes unconscious. Yet it may still influence behavior. How can this be? It seems mysterious, yet everyone wryly recognizes the unconscious motive of the lonely middle-aged spinster who has to look under her bed every night lest a man be hiding there.

The operation of an unconscious motive can be demonstrated experimentally with the aid of hypnosis. The following example is one of several presented by M. H. Erickson:

During hypnosis, the subject was told that he admired and respected Dr. D. very much but that unconsciously he was jealous of him and that because of this jealousy there would be a cutting edge to complimentary remarks which he would make. He was further told that after awakening a conversation would be started with Dr. D. in which he would take part. The subject was then awakened and the conversation begun.

The topic of traveling and its contribution to personal education was mentioned. The subject immediately brought up the fact that Dr. D. had studied both in the

Middle West and in the East and that, having traveled abroad as well, he might well be called cosmopolitan. He himself, he added, would like to travel and get a cosmopolitan education but in the last analysis that was what was being done by any old tramp who traveled from one part of the country to another by stealing rides on freight cars. There followed a discussion of human behavior as it reflected local environments during which the subject remarked that the man who had traveled showed a broader knowledge and better understanding of people and of cultural things; he added, however, that the same thing might possibly be said of any resident of east-side New York.*

Thus, it can be seen that, although the subject was unaware of his jealousy, his behavior was strongly influenced by this unconscious motive.

MOTIVATION AS A BEHAVIORAL DETERMINANT

The studies presented in this chapter suggest that motivation is one of the key factors that determine how a person will behave. Motivation is involved in all kinds of behavior—learning, performing, perceiving, attending, remembering, forgetting, thinking, creating, and feeling. The relationship between motivation and behavior is sometimes complex. A moderate level of motivation may have one effect and an extreme level another. Antagonistic motives may produce a conflict. Some motives may be unconscious. It is only when we learn more about these complex effects of motivation that we will be able to understand human behavior.

* From M. H. Erickson, Experimental demonstrations of the psychopathology of everyday life. *Psychoanal. Quart.*, 1939, 8, 338–353.

Homeostatic Motives

The basic life processes—the production of energy, bodily growth, and the repair of damaged tissue—depend on a delicate set of chemical conditions in the individual cells of any organism. In man, temperature must not vary more than a few degrees from the optimal 98.6 degrees Fahrenheit for any length of time, the water level of the blood and lymph must be more or less constant, chemical constituents of the blood—oxygen, sugar, salts, and so on—must not vary beyond safe limits, and the blood must not become too acid or alkaline. Failure to maintain these conditions leads to a disruption of general functioning and, eventually, death.

3

Biologists believe that organic life began eons ago in warm, tropical, salt seas. There the surrounding environment provided most of the necessary conditions for a unicellular organism. But as living organisms spread out to cooler seas, to fresh water, and to land, special devices were evolved to bring the tropical salt-sea environment along. The individual cells of a complex organism, like a human being, actually live in a warmer-than-tropical, salt-sea bath provided by the blood and the lymphatic fluid.

Most of the special organs of the body operate to maintain the necessary conditions in this tropical sea within our bodies—the internal environment, as it is called. The liver supplies sugar, the lungs furnish oxygen, the kidneys filter out waste products, and so forth. However, the organism is also living in an external environment in which conditions are constantly changing—food supplies are exhausted, water is unavailable, or temperature fluctuates. In spite of these external changes, the organism must maintain an internal stability. Walter B. Cannon called this relatively constant internal state *homeostasis*. If internal conditions change beyond certain limits, a state of *homeostatic disequilibrium* is said to exist and a number of homeostatic mechanisms are thrown into action to remedy the situation.

Many of the homeostatic mechanisms involve internal changes and are of primary concern to the physiologist rather than the psychologist. For example, when the external temperature drops, many animals will burn more fuel and thus keep their body temperature up. Others grow more fur. Some animal mechanisms, however, involve behavioral changes of an instinctive type—thus, small rodents hibernate, some birds migrate south, and, in man, the shivering reflex begins to operate. Finally, the problem becomes even more psychological when the homeostatic disequilibrium gives rise to a motive—a tendency to seek warmth. This is most familiar to us as a feeling of cold and a desire for heat. Such a motive may lead to searching for a cozy nook, learning to build a fire, or inventing a new method of keeping warm, such as an electric blanket.

Karl Lashley gives an example of a homeostatic motive in an organism so simple that the entire process can serve as a pure model. The organism is the tiny Microstoma, about one-half millimeter long. As part of its adaptive system, the Microstoma has small, poisonous stinging cells arranged all over the surface of its body. In defending itself, or capturing prey, the Microstoma discharges these little weapons. Now, the Microstoma does not manufacture these cells but gets them from another microscopic animal, the Hydra. It eats Hydra, digests out the stinging cells in its stomach, and transports them to the skin. When the stinging cells are used up, the Microstoma eats Hydra greedily but then loses its appetite as the concentration of stinging cells on the body surface reaches an appropriate concentration. Lashley points out that the major problems of motivation are here in one-half a millimeter—the need, the specific consummatory activity, and the satiation.

A number of motives important to human beings are usually classified as homeostatic. Hunger and thirst are the clearest examples of motives associated with an internal deficit of substances needed for bodily functions. Actually both of these motives are more complex than they seem. Hunger can be broken down into several subhungers since the body needs specific substances such as protein, carbohydrates, fats, minerals, and vitamins. So, too, thirst involves both a need for water and a need for salt in order to maintain the proper salt-sea bath. Breathing motivation usually insures the supply of oxygen needed for homeostatic processes.

A number of other motives are important in homeostasis because they avoid potentially dangerous environmental conditions rather than remedy an internal deficit. Thus, we have the avoidance of temperature extremes, bright light, loud sounds, electric shock, and any pain-producing stimuli. These conditions may cause tissue damage and indirectly affect homeostasis.

Finally, there is a set of motives that arise from the bodily processes and activities of a person himself. The simplest of these are the eliminative motives—the tendency to breath out eliminates CO_2, while urination and defecation eliminate other waste products. General bodily activity eventually produces fatigue and sleepiness. The motives to rest and sleep apparently operate to anticipate and avoid injury to the body through excessive activity. Resting when fatigued permits the removal of waste products like lactic acid from the muscles. The exact homeostatic function of sleep is not known. It has been suggested that everyday tensions are discharged through dreams, but sleep may also have a more specific homeostatic function.

In general, conditions that create a homeostatic imbalance apparently give rise to a variety of psychological motives, the goals of which are the restoration or maintenance of internal equilibrium. Such homeostatic equilibrium is important for biological survival. This homeostatic model is extremely logical and has had a great impact on psychological thought. Some psychologists maintain that homeostasis, directly or indirectly, is the basis for all human motivation. The ability of the model to account for complex human motives for achievement, affection, self-esteem, and so on has been challenged, of course, but beyond this the question has been raised whether homeostasis fully explains even motives like hunger, thirst, and pain.

In this chapter, we shall first examine the nature of drive—the arousal of a psychological motive—and then the nature of reward—the termination of a psychological motive. We shall use hunger as the main example throughout because more is known about this motive than any of the others. Our chief concern will be the adequacy of the homeostatic model to explain hunger and similar motives.

THE NATURE OF DRIVE

According to the homeostatic theory, a psychological drive—with its many effects on activity, goal selection, and conscious want—stems from an internal disequilibrium. Thus, Clark Hull, an influential psychological theorist, equates psychological drive with physiological need. This equation seems to describe the situation quite accurately in a simple organism like the Microstoma, but the process appears to be more complex in the higher species. In a complex organism, a number of mechanisms intervenes between a need in the tissues of the body and the organization of goal-seeking behavior. First, we shall examine closely the processes and mechanisms involved in the hunger drive.

Then, we shall raise the question of the relationship between a physiological need and a psychological drive. Finally, we shall discuss the stimulating or energizing character of a psychological drive.

Hunger

For most of us, hunger means the state of our stomachs—the pangs of hunger. The importance of stomach contractions in hunger was demonstrated years ago by W. B. Cannon and A. L. Washburn. They devised an ingenious device consisting of a balloon, which is swallowed by the subject, and a tube leading out of the mouth attached to a recording device. A stomach contraction would squeeze the balloon and be recorded. Experiments showed that there was a close correspondence between the contractions of the stomach and the conscious experience of hunger.

Nevertheless, subsequent studies have shown that hunger is not dependent on these stomach contractions. People who have had their stomachs removed still experience hunger. In several experiments with animals, all the nerves between the stomach and the brain were severed. Yet the animals ate normally and did well in learning mazes to get food. Therefore, it appears that signals from the stomach are not necessary for hunger.

It is more likely that the chemical state of the blood directly affects the brain. The level of sugar in the blood may be a factor, as shown by the increase in eating following an injection of insulin, although various attempts to correlate blood sugar levels directly with hunger have been unsuccessful. We do know, though, that the blood of hungry and satiated animals is different. If blood from a hungry rat is injected into a satiated one, he starts eating. Still, very little is known about the nature of the chemical factors in the blood that affect hunger. They may include the level of various nutriments or some group of hormones secreted by different bodily organs.

Although the exact nature of the blood factors responsible for hunger is not known, the part of the brain most sensitive to them is now firmly established. It is the hypothalamus, a tiny area at the base of the brain, near the pituitary gland, with a rich blood supply. This small area appears to be important in nearly all the physiological motives and emotions.

In the case of hunger, there is a tiny part of the hypothalamus known as the "feeding area." In an experimental animal, a slender electrode can be inserted into this area and fixed in place. A mild electric current can be used to stimulate the "feeding area." When this is done, even when the animal is satiated, eating behavior is produced. Furthermore, stimulation of this area will produce an increase in the performance of a learned response, such as bar-pressing, to get a food reward. This is true even when a food-satiated, but thirsty, animal has to leave a drinking spout to make the food response. Thus, it can be seen that electrical stimulation of the "feeding area" of the hypothalamus produces a condition very close to normal hunger. On the other hand, destroying this area eliminates eating. Therefore, this particular region in the hypothalamus may be considered the chief mechanism controlling the arousal of hunger.

Although there is little doubt about the importance of the hypothalamus in hunger, other parts of the brain are also involved. For example, it is well established that hunger is also aroused by the sight, smell, and taste of food. These environmental stimuli are transmitted, not directly to the hypothalamus, but to the cerebrum, the outer part of the brain, which is usually thought to be the mechanism for the higher mental processes.

The relationships among the various mechanisms in hunger are shown in Figure 3. At the basis of the whole process are cellular metabolism and the need for calories to produce heat and do the work of the body. In the case of the need for sugar, or glucose, the cellular absorption of sugar from the blood sets the stage for hormonal or direct neural stimulation of the brain by the sugar-depleted blood supply, thereby activating the hypothalamic hunger-drive mechanism and giving rise to sensations of hunger in the cerebrum. The hypothalamic mechanisms, in addition to the blood factors, stimulate the stomach to contract, providing a secondary source of hunger, the sensation of hunger pangs. The hypothalamic and other brain mechanisms also activate the eating responses, the actual eating being dependent on the presence of food. The role of external stimulation is also shown by the fact that food helps to arouse hunger.

Does this series of mechanisms extend to all the nutritional deficiencies in the body? Recall that hunger really consists of a set of subhungers for various specific substances. Does each of the specific deficiencies lead to a seeking for food rich in the needed substance?

As a general tendency, hunger for various substances varies with the specific needs of the organism. This tendency has sometimes been called the "wisdom of the body." Wild animals, for example, tend to select food in accordance with the needs of the body. This effect has also been demonstrated in the laboratory with what are called "cafeteria-feeding" experiments. In a well-known study, C. M. Davis fed human infants with the cafeteria technique for several years after weaning. A number of dishes and glasses of food were placed before each child at mealtime and he was allowed to eat as much or as little of each as he pleased. The children thrived on this regime. Although they went on occasional binges, they selected a very well-balanced diet over the long run. One child even cured himself of rickets by eating large amounts of cod liver oil.

These results should be interpreted with caution. The foods offered the children were simple and pure. If highly desirable items like ice cream and chocolate eclairs were included, the results might have been different. Habit

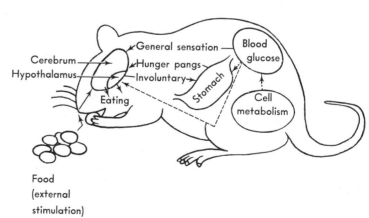

Figure 3. Physiological mechanisms of hunger. Dotted lines indicate biochemical or hormonal effects; solid lines, nervous stimulation. This diagrams the ingestion of foods from which glucose is obtained. It would be far more complex if it included all foodstuffs. (After J. P. Scott. Animal Behavior. Chicago: Univ. of Chicago Press, 1958.)

also plays a large role in determining preferences. In one study, animals deficient in sugar learned to prefer the sugar sucrose. Later on, when the animals were protein-deficient but not sugar-deficient, they continued the preference for sugar. On the human level, habit and social imitation play even a greater role. It is for these reasons that most medical authorities have criticized the appealing idea that children can be left free to select their own diets.

The need for a specific substance was most clearly demonstrated in an experiment by Curt Richter and his associates. Rats were fed a diet deficient in Vitamin B and then given a choice of several drinking bottles. The rats very quickly selected the bottle containing a solution of pure Vitamin B. Once they had a taste of it, it was difficult to stop their drinking—they would hang on with paws and teeth if the bottle was withdrawn.

This effect should not be overgeneralized, however, since many other vitamins, particularly A and D, are not preferred when the animal is deprived of them. Furthermore, even the Vitamin B has to be in strong concentration for an animal to detect it. If the concentration of Vitamin B is not strong enough to taste, a preference can still be established by labelling the needed vitamin with a distinctive flavor. But later on, if the Vitamin B is withdrawn, the animal continues to show a preference for the old flavor. Again we see the importance of habit.

Various endocrine and hormonal changes in the body affect appetite for various foods. For example, rats deprived of their pancreas might be expected to develop diabetes. They do not because they eat very little sugar and get their calories from fats. Probably the most familiar example is a pregnant or lactating mother. Because of the needs of the growing fetus or nursing infant, the mother must have more minerals, such as sodium, calcium, and phosphorus, and also more protein and fat. Additional sugar is not needed. Thus, pregnant and lactating female rats prefer foods rich in the necessary ingredients. Afterwards a normal diet is preferred. Pregnant women also show changes in appetite but are more influenced by habit. They frequently eat too much sugar along with the necessary nutriments and put on excessive weight during pregnancy.

Thus, although there is a primitive sort of "wisdom of the body" and a set of physiological mechanisms to translate bodily needs into action, these are severely limited. Not all bodily needs result in a specific hunger. Taste preferences and habit often outweigh the physiological needs of the body. In man, cultural values appear to play an important role in dietary selection.

The physiological mechanisms of a number of other drives are similar to those of hunger. Areas in the hypothalamus have been shown to be important in thirst, sleep and wakefulness, and temperature regulation. Hypothalamic mechanisms appear to be sensitive to various conditions in the body *before* real emergency states are reached. They *anticipate* deficiencies, exhaustion, or injury. However, they do not always operate in a fully homeostatic fashion.

Physiological Need versus Psychological Drive

The concept of homeostasis is based on the idea that physiological needs produce a disequilibrium that requires adjustment. For many scientists, a psychological drive is an extension of the internal mechanisms responding to the physiological need, and we have seen some excellent examples of that. Nevertheless, there are reasons against the simple equation of psychological drive with physiological need.

First of all, as we have seen in this chapter, there are a number of physiological needs that do not result in psychological drives. There may be a number of vitamin deficiencies that a person is unaware of or that do not affect his goals. A more dramatic example is the failure of oxygen deficiency to motivate a person. Breathing in normally serves to provide the body with oxygen. However, the drive is for breathing in *air,* not *oxygen* specifically. Thus, although the body requires oxygen, the psychological motive is fulfilled if the individual breathes in air containing little or no oxygen. This rarely happens in normal life but can lead to death for airmen or submariners who have to leave the natural environment. On the negative side, we may breathe in the deadly poison carbon monoxide without any motivating effect. It is clear, then, that not all physiological needs have a counterpart in psychological motivation.

The arousal of a psychological drive also appears to be somewhat independent of physiological need. Most psychological drives are anticipatory. That is, the organism becomes hungry long before the tissues are actually depleted of necessary materials. At high levels of physiological need, the psychological drive may disappear. For example, men who are totally deprived of food lose their hunger drive and have no conscious desire to eat.

Another difference between physiological need and psychological drive is that the latter may be influenced by learning. The learning conditions may result in a nonhomeostatic condition. For example, a person may have learned in his childhood relationship with his mother that eating reduced anxiety. Whenever he feels anxious, now, he is ravenous and can reduce his anxiety by eating. This may lead to a nonhomeostatic obesity. Similarly, there was a case of a man who typically fell asleep whenever he began to feel angry. In psychotherapy, it was discovered that as a child, whenever he became angry or irritable, his parents interpreted the cause as fatigue and sent him to bed. Thus, he learned to feel sleepy whenever he became angry.

It should be noted that social factors may influence animal as well as human drive. For example, hens fed in groups eat more than when they are fed alone. Human beings, though, are even more subject to social influence. In general, it appears that the dependence of drives on homeostasis decreases as we go up the evolutionary scale. The motivation of a very simple organism like the Microstoma appears to be directly responsive to physiological needs, the hen less so, and man least of all.

Therefore, the simple equation of a physiological need or homeostatic imbalance with psychological drive is not justified. Although it is obvious that drives like hunger, thirst, and so on are related to physiological needs, they are not perfectly responsive to them. More is involved in psychological drives than homeostatic imbalance.

Drive Stimuli versus Drive Energization

For a number of psychological theorists, drive operates on an organism by a general energization of all responses and activities. The Microstoma provides a good example of how a particular drive mobilizes the energy of the entire organism. At a higher evolutionary level, it has been shown that hungry rats will engage in more maze exploration than satiated ones. Nevertheless, there are many other instances in which a drive condition does not result in increased activity. When hunger is increased beyond a certain optimal point, general activity begins to decrease.

Several theorists have suggested that rather than resulting in increased overt activity, a drive functions to produce an internal state of arousal. Thirsty rats, for example, show an increased heart rate when pressing a bar to get water, even when their bar-pressing has fallen off in frequency due to high drive. Even this generalization has been challenged, however. Drive conditions like heat, fatigue, and sleep-deprivation appear to lead to a lowered level of internal arousal.

All these difficulties have led a number of psychologists to question the energizing concept of drive. But if drive is not a general internal arousal, what is it? One answer is that a drive may simply be a stimulus—either internal or external. The external sources of drive, such as the pain from electric shock, fit in with a drive-stimulus position very well. It has been shown, for example, that different intensities of shock can be discriminated the way other stimuli can.

The important question is whether internal drives can also be shown to have the properties of a stimulus. Since one of the chief characteristics of a stimulus is that, within limits, it can be differentiated from other stimuli, then stimuli associated with internal drives should be discriminable. This has been demonstrated in experiments by Clark Hull, Robert Leeper, and others. Rats can be trained to run down the stem of a T-maze and turn one way on hungry days to get food and the other on thirsty days to get water. Similarly, an animal can be trained to turn one way when mildly hungry and another when very hungry.

Thus, the drive-stimulus theorists would assume that a characteristic set of stimuli would be associated with each drive. These would be external for some drives and internal for others. Increasing drive would mean increasing the intensity of these stimuli, their number, or their probability of occurrence. For some of these theorists, reward would consist of the reduction of these stimuli—escaping shock reduces the shock stimulus; eating may inhibit the stimuli from the stomach and hypothalamus.

These theorists still have to explain why certain drives sometimes do have what appears to be an energizing effect on behavior. The way they account for this appearance is to assume that general activity and internal arousal consist of a series of learned reactions to internal and external cues, both drive stimuli and neutral stimuli. For example, food-deprived animals may not show an activity increase until the experimenter turns on a light or a sound. This may be the result of learned connections between stimuli and responses.

The issue has not yet been resolved. At the present time we can say that drives like hunger involve internal stimuli. These may be the signals from the stomach, bloodstream, and hypothalamus. External stimuli, like the sight of food, are also involved. Under some conditions, a drive may also involve a generalized arousal of the entire organism in addition to specific reactions to signals. The physiological basis for internal arousal will be discussed in Chapter 5, which is on emotional motives.

Just as the homeostatic model predicts that a condition producing a deviation from equilibrium produces a drive, it also predicts that a condition returning the body to homeostatic balance *satiates* the drive and functions as a *reward*. Thus, Clark Hull equates *reward* with *need-reduction*. For some time there has been a question about this equation. For example, Neal E. Miller has pointed out that the effects of a small pellet of food on need-reduction must be limited and delayed. Yet, it acts as a strong reward for a hungry animal. In addition, an animal may become satiated and cease bar-pressing long before the tissue need is changed. There seems to be something more involved than direct need-reduction. Let us examine the nature of the satiation and reward processes involved in hunger in some detail. Then we shall examine several examples of reward that have nothing to do with the reduction of a physiological need.

Hunger

We have discussed the physiological mechanisms underlying the arousal of hunger. Now, what about the mechanisms for reducing hunger, producing satiation, and having a rewarding effect? From a purely biological point of view, the process is completed only when the necessary biochemical substances reach the cells. This would be several hours after eating and could hardly account for the fairly rapid satiation and rewarding effects of eating. There must be physiological mechanisms that *anticipate* the reduction of the biological need.

The mechanism of central importance in reducing hunger is also found in the hypothalamus. The satiation mechanism is in a part of that organ separate from the feeding area. It apparently operates to stop eating behavior. If this mechanism is destroyed, a condition known as hyperphasia is produced—the animal will overeat and become obese. On the other hand, electrical stimulation of this area reduces eating. However, Neal E. Miller and his associates, in an attempt to show that stimulation of this area would be rewarding, found that the stimulation itself was aversive to the animal. The animals would hesitantly press a bar to turn it on and then turn it off quickly. Hopefully, the complexity of these mechanisms will be clarified by future research. There is little doubt, however, that there is some sort of satiation mechanism in the hypothalamus.

The question then arises, what are the sources of information that influence the hypothalamic satiation mechanism? There are three main possibilities—the taste receptors in the mouth, the distention of the stomach, and the biochemical state of the blood. The role of taste and stomach factors in hunger-reduction was demonstrated by Martin Kohn, using a stomach-fistula method. In this procedure, a plastic tube is inserted into the stomach of a rat, passed through the body wall, run under the skin, and brought out at the back of the neck where the rat cannot scratch it. Food can then be injected directly into the stomach or eaten normally. Kohn used the rate of pressing a bar to get food as a measure of hunger. Before the bar-pressing test, the animals either received a milk mixture by mouth (normal eating), had the same amount injected directly into the stomach, or had a control injection of normal saline (slightly salty water) into the stomach. The greatest reduction in hunger occurred when food is taken by mouth, but food injected directly into the stomach also reduced hunger. Both taste and stomach stimulation, then, are involved in hunger-reduction.

Subsequently, Neal E. Miller and his associates showed that a rat would learn a response in which the reward is milk injected directly into the stomach. In a simple, T-shaped maze, animals were given the milk injection if they turned left and a saline injection if they turned right. After about 30 trials, the rats learned to go to the side where they received the milk. This is a little slower than when the reward is by mouth, but there is no question that food injected directly into the stomach is a sufficient reward for learning.

It would also seem logical that a nutritive substance injected directly into the blood stream would serve as a reward. This has proven to be technically difficult to achieve, but Randall M. Chambers succeeded in demonstrating such a phenomenon in the rabbit. A tube very similar to the apparatus used in hospitals for intravenous feeding was attached to the ear vein of each rabbit. Testing was done in an apparatus with several floor plates. When a rabbit sat on one plate, glucose flowed into the vein; on another, a nonnutritive sweet substance; on still others, normal saline. The results showed that the rabbits learned to sit on the plate associated with the injection of the nutritive glucose sugar and spent more time there. This was not true of the nonnutritive sweet substance nor of the saline. Subsequent eating tests also indicated that rabbits receiving glucose injections were less hungry.

How does the glucose injection reduce hunger? It is possible, but not likely, that the tissue needs are immediately reduced by the presence of sugar. The sugar may have altered other chemical substances in the blood. It is also possible that the taste receptors in the tongue may have been affected. When human beings are given an injection of glucose in the arm, they report a sweet taste in the mouth seconds later. Finally, the glucose in the blood may have stimulated the satiation mechanism in the hypothalamus.

This entire area of study is new, with research findings emerging constantly. Probably within a decade we shall know a great deal more about the physiological basis of reward and satiation. From what we know now, the reduction of hunger involves a multiplicity of mechanisms—in the mouth, stomach, and blood stream—most likely coordinated by the brain, particularly the hypothalamus.

Considerably less is known about the satiation and rewarding processes in drives other than hunger. Recent research suggests that thirst is somewhat similar. Thirst can be reduced by water taken in the mouth, introduced into the stomach, or injected directly into the hypothalamus. Other rewards also probably involve a number of peripheral signals that affect brain mechanisms.

Rewards Independent of Need-Reduction

So far we have seen that a number of factors are involved in the reduction of a drive like hunger. Signals from the taste buds in the mouth, the distention of the stomach, and the chemical state of the blood have an effect on the satiation mechanism in the hypothalamus. Furthermore, food in the mouth, stomach, and blood-stream operate as rewards. These satiating and rewarding effects are seen long before there has been a change in the physiological needs of the individual cells. Nevertheless, food eventually does reduce physiological needs, so the results are somewhat inconclusive.

There are also rewards that do not reduce a physiological need at any time. The clearest case is that of saccharine. Saccharine is a chemical substance that tastes sweet, and is desirable, but does not provide energy and passes through the body unchanged. This is why people on a diet find saccharine helpful as a substitute for sugar. This nonnutritive substance has been shown to be a strong reward for animals in learning situations.

Although it is clear that saccharine does not reduce a physiological need, it does, in fact, reduce the hunger drive. Neal E. Miller, Warren W. Roberts, and this author demonstrated that this is so by prefeeding rats with a saccharine solution and then testing for hunger. Animals prefed with saccharine ate less food and pressed a bar for food reinforcement less frequently than control animals. The effect is entirely dependent on taste, which suggests that direct sensory stimulation can affect a drive without reducing a physiological need.

The independence of reward and punishment from physiological need was most dramatically demonstrated by the discovery that directly stimulating certain areas of the brain can be rewarding or punishing. James Olds and his associates implanted electrodes in the area of the brain of animals that includes the forward part of the hypothalamus and closely related parts of the *limbic system* of the brain. (The limbic system is explained and illustrated in Chapter 5.) An apparatus was constructed so that an animal could press a bar to turn on the current. This is shown in Figure 4. This self-administered electrical current has been found to be highly rewarding for rats, cats and monkeys. Animals learn to press the bar even for quite high voltages and appear never to tire of it. If the source of current is disconnected, the animals show an extinction effect just as they do when food pellets are discontinued.

There is some evidence suggesting that self-stimulation of the brain in the rewarding area operates by producing a sensation of pleasure. Some people have even gone so far as to speak of a "pleasure" center in the brain. The evidence for this claim comes from studies of a few volunteer terminal cancer patients who have had electrodes implanted in the rewarding area. They typically reported a pleasurable sensation, a decrease in tension, and an increased alertness, although a few patients showed increased tension.

The parts of the limbic system more to the rear of the brain appear to be a punishing area. Neal E. Miller and his associates have demonstrated that animals will learn to rotate a wheel to *turn off* electrical stimulation to this area. When the electrical stimulation was preceded by a tone, the animals learned to avoid the current. Thus, this rear portion of the limbic system is involved in both fear and pain.

Although electrical stimulation of the limbic system does not result in the reduction of a physiological need, the rewarding effect is not unrelated to drive conditions. Several studies have shown that animals will perform for the brain stimulation more rapidly when they are hungry. This suggests that the rewarding area has some connection with ordinary hunger. Olds found that

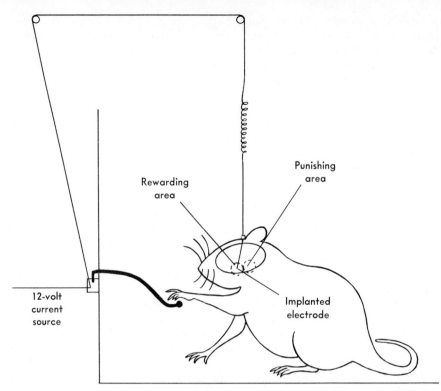

Figure 4. Brain self-stimulation. An animal with an electrode implanted in the "rewarding" area of the brain will learn to press a bar in a Skinner Box to turn on a moderate electric current. The depression of the bar turns on the current, which is carried by a light, flexible wire held high above the Skinner Box. Stimulation in the "punishing" area is aversive to the rat. (Modified from J. Olds. Physiological mechanisms of reward. In M. R. Jones (ed.). Nebraska symposium on motivation. *Lincoln: University of Nebraska Press, 1955.)*

certain points in the rewarding area were more rewarding when the animals were deprived of food and others when the animals were given sexual hormones which presumably increased sexual motivation. Thus, it appears that these brain mechanisms are tied in with various drives. Even so, the important thing to keep in mind is that the rewarding effect of the brain stimulation is not dependent on the reduction of a physiological need.

NEW IDEAS ABOUT HOMEOSTATIC MOTIVES

The result of all the evidence mentioned in this chapter is that the relation between physiological need and psychological motivation is exceedingly complex. Certainly, drives are not simply reflections of homeostatic imbalance, and rewards are not simply restorations of imbalance. A drive like hunger may be aroused without a physiological need and not all nutritional needs result in hunger. The taste of a substance may reduce hunger, and electrical stimulation of the brain may be rewarding to a hungry animal. It is clear that homeostasis does not explain adequately either drive or reward. What other explanations are possible?

One alternative is Neal E. Miller's basic distinction between a physiological need and a psychological motive. The two may be correlated but they are not the same thing. A physiological need is a strictly biological process involving the homeostatic imbalance we have described. A psychological drive is a set of stimuli aroused by psychological conditions like going without food for a period, smelling a sizzling steak, or feeling hungry when insecure. So, too, the reduction of a drive stimulus is different from the reduction of a need. A drive like hunger can be reduced by the taste of food or a nonnutritive substance like saccharine.

A second idea comes from the hedonic theorists like Paul Young and David McClelland. They explain reward on the basis of pleasure. The strong rewarding effects of the nonnutritive, sweet-tasting saccharine and of the pleasurable brain stimulation offer support for the hedonic position. The effects of drive conditions like hunger would be explained as enhancing the pleasurable qualities of different rewards.

Finally, a reasonable hypothesis, presented by several people, is that psychological drives and rewards are mediated by brain mechanisms dependent as much on external stimulation as on internal drive stimuli. Pleasure and pain may be the direct means for influencing the behavior of a person. These mechanisms have the side-effect of reducing physiological need a certain percentage of the time. The brain mechanisms probably evolved slowly and tend to increase the chances of survival. It is possible that, in the future, other brain mechanisms will be evolved in the face of changing environmental conditions. One geneticist believes that men could be bred to sense atomic radiation and respond to it as an aversive drive. In the meantime, we can classify hunger, thirst, and so on as homeostatic motives because they are relevant to physiological need, but we should also keep in mind that they are mediated by brain mechanisms not perfectly correlated with internal homeostatic conditions.

Sexual Motivation   Sigmund Freud shocked
his Victorian world when he insisted that sexuality is a
powerful motivating force in human behavior, lurking
behind the scenes of genteel civilized life, and erupting
into marital tensions, neurotic symptoms, and seemingly
innocent dreams. We like to think of ourselves as being
considerably more sophisticated now, but the topic still
leads to embarrassment or sniggering. The public reaction
to Alfred Kinsey's monumental statistical study of American sexual behavior could hardly be called detached—it
was condemned as a corrupting influence and endorsed as
a license for all sorts of behavior. Such attitudes are what

4

make a sober scientific study of sexual motivation so difficult to undertake.

What is the nature of sexual motivation? To begin with, sexual motivation seems different from the motives we discussed in the last chapter. No opparent homeostatic function is involved. An important biological function is served by sexual motivation, of course, but it is the preservation of the species rather than the survival of the individual. Among other things, then, our analysis of sexual motivation will illustrate the limitation of homeostasis as a model for all motives. We shall first discuss the physiological mechanisms for sexual behavior, then the nature of sex as a motive, and finally the development of sexual motivation and its role in personality.

PHYSIOLOGICAL BASIS OF SEXUAL BEHAVIOR

Sexual behavior, in both the male and female, depends on a combination of internal and external factors. The internal factors are hormones and brain mechanisms whereas the external ones are learned and unlearned environmental stimuli. At one time, sexual behavior was thought to depend almost exclusively on sexual hormones, but recent research has indicated the importance of the other factors. There are evolutionary differences in the relative importance of these factors in sexual behavior, as we shall see. We shall discuss, first, the role of hormones, then turn to brain mechanisms and environmental stimuli.

Sex Hormones

The male testes, in addition to producing the sperm necessary for reproduction, secrete the male hormones (androgens) and a small amount of the female hormones (estrogens). Before puberty the production of both is quite low, but as a male reaches puberty, the supply of androgens is dramatically increased. The increase in androgens not only stimulates the development of the secondary sex characteristics but is also correlated with a marked increase in sexual interest and activity. Sexual decline in later years is probably due to a decrease in hormone production.

A more direct demonstration of the effect of hormones on male sexual behavior is provided by experimental castration. In this procedure, the chief source of male hormones is eliminated by surgically removing the testes. Although the general effect of castration is to diminish sexual behavior, this statement must be modified in several ways. First, the effect is much more marked when the castration is done before puberty—the method used by the ancients to provide eunuchs to guard the harem. Second, the effect of castration depends on the evolutionary stage of the species. Lower mammals, such as rats and guinea pigs, show a rapid and complete decline in sexual activity after castration; larger mammals, such as dogs, may retain potency for several years; and primates, like chimpanzees, may show undiminished sexual activity for an indeterminate period.

As one might suspect, the situation on the human level is the most complex of all. Some men report a loss or marked decline in sexual interest and capacity after castration. Others report a continued high level of performance for as long as 30 years. Human sexuality seems to be more greatly influenced by psychological factors. There have been some clinical reports of men suffering from impotence who were convinced that the cause was glandular insufficiency. Several became potent immediately after being told that their hormone level was normal. Sexual behavior that has been reduced by castration can be restored by the administration of hormones, as has been demonstrated in a variety of species, including man.

Female sexual behavior is also influenced by hormones, although the relationship is a bit more complex. Female sexual activity, as well as the development of secondary sex characteristics, is increased at puberty by the female hormones, which are produced by the ovaries along with a small amount of male hormones. However, puberty also marks the beginning of the estrual, or fertility, cycle in females.

The female fertility cycle, which in the human being lasts about four weeks, is controlled by a complex interaction between the hormones of the ovaries and the pituitary. Briefly, during the first two weeks of the cycle one ovary prepares an egg for fertilization and both ovaries secrete the female hormone, estrogen. Estrogen prepares the uterus for implantation and also appears to have a tendency to arouse sexual interest. Psychoanalytic observations show that women tend to have erotic dreams during this phase of the cycle. In about two weeks, ovulation occurs—the fertile egg starts its journey to the uterus. At the same time, the ovaries begin to secrete progesterone—the maternal hormone, which further prepares the uterus for implantation and indirectly prepares the mammary glands for nursing. During the second half of the fertility cycle, when progesterone is dominant, women have dreams with more maternal themes.

In lower mammals, the sexual motive of the female is closely bound to the fertility cycle. The female is receptive only during the period of ovulation. At a higher evolutionary level, the sexual behavior of the female is not so strongly determined by the fertility cycle. Monkeys and apes have been observed to copulate during all phases of the fertility cycle, although ovulation is still the period of greatest sexual excitement and activity. Female apes may also be more selective in their sex partners, showing responsiveness to one male and aversion to another. All this points to a lessening of hormonal control, with the emergence of social and emotional factors.

Finally, on the human level, the hormonal influence over feminine sexual activity seems to be overshadowed by the psychological conditions. Women frequently engage in sexual relations on a regular basis, at all times of the fertility cycle. This may be due partly to the sexual desire of the male, but there is evidence suggesting that women are responsive to some degree at all times. There is a rhythm of sexual desire in most women, but according to several questionnaire studies, this rarely coincides with ovulation. Most women report their most intense desire shortly before or shortly after menstruation. Since the dreams still show a hormonal influence, it is possible that the reversal in the human female is due to an inhibition during the estrual peak because of a fear of pregnancy.

The removal of the ovaries, female castration, has effects similar to those found with male castration. In lower animals, such an operation completely abolishes sexual behavior in the female, and the male no longer is attracted.

Chimpanzees and other apes may continue to show sexual responsiveness after the ovaries are removed, although the usual cycle of responsiveness is abolished and the general level of sexual activity is low. On the other hand, women who have had their ovaries removed or who have passed through the menopause do not necessarily lose their sexual desire. In fact, many show an increased sexual interest, possibly because the fear of pregnancy is eliminated. Here, too, the supply of hormones from the ovaries is not crucial to sexual behavior in the human female.

Neural Mechanisms

As we have seen, hormones do not account for all of sexual behavior, particularly at the higher evolutionary levels. This leaves the nervous system as the primary physiological basis of the sex motive. We shall consider four neural mechanisms in sexual activity—sensory receptors, spinal reflexes, hypothalamic integration, and cortical influences.

Tactile, or touch, stimulation of sensory receptors is an important part of sexual arousal and release. To some extent, all the tactile receptors of the body may contribute to erotic arousal. Nonetheless, the chief concentration of sensory receptors involved in sexual arousal is in the genitalia—specifically, the glans penis at the tip of the male organ and the clitoris in the female.

That a number of the basic sexual reflexes are controlled by the lower spinal cord has been demonstrated for animals from frog to man. The spinal reflexes include erection, pelvic movements, and ejaculation in the male. This has been observed in wounded war veterans, paraplegics, whose spinal cords have been severed in battle. Paraplegics cannot voluntarily move or receive sensation from their lower limbs. Yet there was one case of a paraplegic who succeeded in impregnating his wife showing that spinal reflexes are sufficient for minimal sexual activity.

In an intact organism, sexual arousal and behavior are chiefly organized in an area of the hypothalamus. Again we see the importance of this tiny area of the brain for motivational phenomena, for destruction of the relevant area in the hypothalamus eliminates sexual behavior. This sexual area of the hypothalamus appears to organize the more complex parts of sexual behavior. For example, although the genital reflexes remain, a female cat with a hypothalamic injury does not show typical crouching behavior with a male.

The role played by tactile receptors, spinal reflexes, and hypothalamic organization is not essentially different in various animals including man. These parts of the nervous system are quite similar in the different species of mammals. The great evolutionary change is in the size and importance of the cerebral cortex, the outer layer of the brain, which is extremely large and complex in man. It is usually thought to mediate the functions of assessing environmental stimuli, learning, thinking, and organizing complex activities. How is the cortex related to sexual behavior?

The effect of taking out various amounts of cortical tissue on sexual behavior was studied by Frank Beach. He removed up to 75 per cent of the cortex in male rats and observed their behavior. The number of rats copulating during a test decreased as more and more cortex was removed. Sexual behavior was totally abolished after two-thirds of the cortex was gone. No one particular area of the cortex was essential since the cortex tends to act as a whole. The role of the cortex in the sexual behavior of the female rat is not so marked.

The most significant result of the cortex-removal studies is the demonstration that the cortex is proportionately more important as we go up the evolutionary scale. The sexual capacity of lower mammals is not seriously disturbed by cortical destruction. Higher animals, and probably man, are much more seriously impaired by cortical destruction. As we indicated, genital reflexes depend on the lower spinal cord and the execution of the more complex sexual patterns depends on the hypothalamic mechanism. The destruction of the cortex serves to interfere with the arousal of sexual interest by environmental stimuli. This suggests that at the higher evolutionary levels environmental stimuli play a greater role in sexual behavior.

Environmental Stimuli

According to Frank Beach, the popular image of the sexually aroused stag roaming through the woods in search of a mate is not entirely accurate. The stag is not continuously excited. When he meets a receptive female in his ordinary wanderings, he may or may not be aroused. Given the proper hormonal conditions, the critical factor in sexual arousal is the environmental stimulus—the sight, sound, and smell of the receptive female.

The appropriate stimuli vary considerably from species to species. The stimulation sometimes is chemical—as in the male gypsy moth who is attracted by a secretion of the female. The male cricket chirps and the male frog bellows to attract fertile females. Fishes show a definite courtship pattern, the male being attracted by the color or shape of the female with eggs. Birds show a number of courtship patterns including the strutting of the peacock and the charging of the pigeon. One of these patterns has provided an inspiration for human beings—the billing and cooing of certain birds. Billing consists of interlocking beaks and moving heads up and down, accompanied by the cooing vocalization.

There are important evolutionary trends in the nature of the environmental stimuli that are sexually arousing. Lower animals are aroused by very limited and specific environmental stimuli—for example, certain odors in the case of the rabbit. Higher mammals depend on more complex and variable stimuli. The human being is the most complex of all and shows a strong effect of learning in his response to sexual stimuli.

In human beings, cultural learning plays a vital part in determining what aspects of the other person will be attractive. Anthropological studies have revealed that conceptions of feminine beauty vary considerably from one society to another. In some societies, slim, lightly rounded women are considered most appealing, while in others quite plump, even somewhat obese women have all the honors. The attractiveness of males frequently depends less on physical characteristics than on social features, such as their dominance in the group.

Human sexual behavior is also influenced by another product of social learning—internalized, symbolic stimuli such as thoughts, fantasies, and dreams. These are influenced by environmental stimuli and very likely originate in past learning experiences. The fantasies stimulated by books, motion pictures, and the competitive bragging of peers may contribute to the preoccupation of the adolescent boy with sexual matters.

Interrelationship of Factors

How are all these factors interrelated? The various stimuli from the sex partner—sight, smell, and touch—operate through brain mechanisms to arouse sexual interest. The cortex is presumably the source of learned influences, whereas innate reactions are mediated more by the hypothalamus and parts of the limbic system. Sexual performance would depend on genital stimulation and spinal reflexes. Hormones probably operate by sensitizing brain mechanisms and genital reflexes.

The relative importance of these factors depends on evolutionary level. As we go up the evolutionary scale, the influence of hormones decreases and the learned reactions mediated by the cortex become more significant. Environmental stimuli are important for all species, but at the lower levels sexual behavior is controlled by a narrow range of stereotyped innate stimuli, whereas at the higher levels the effective stimuli are more variable and more influenced by learning. For man, the sexual motive is primarily a psychological phenomenon, dependent more on cultural learning and internal, symbolic processes than on hormonal and innate patterns of stimulation.

SEX AS A MOTIVE

So far we have seen that sexual behavior depends on a combination of internal and external factors. We have also seen that there have been important changes in the nature of sexual behavior during evolution. The question that now arises is whether sex functions as a motive. By this we mean, does sex direct and control behavior, produce new learning, and function as a reward? We are also interested in whether it follows the pattern of deprivation and satiation we have seen in the homeostatic motives.

Sex as a Reward for Learning

As you will recall from the discussion in the introductory chapter, one of the key definitions of a motive is that it directs behavior towards a specific goal and such a goal serves as a reward for the learning of new responses. Learning for a sexual reward was extensively studied by Jerome Kagan. He trained male rats to run down a T-maze, the arms of which led to two circular arenas, with a receptive female in one of them. The rats were able to learn the correct turn when the reward was copulation to completion. This shows that a complete sexual experience functions as a reward for new learning.

Kagan went on to study the rewarding effects of partial sexual behavior. Now, the sexual pattern of the male rat requires a little explanation. The male is attracted by the courting run of the receptive female, mounts her, and inserts the penis. The insertion of the penis is called an *intromission,* but a single intromission is not usually sufficient for an *ejaculation*. The male backs off after each intromission and then resumes the chase. After several intromissions, ejaculation is achieved and the sexual behavior ceases. Kagan studied the effects of just mounting or intromission. Male rats were allowed to mount a female whose vagina had been sewn up so that intromission was impossible. In another condition, animals were allowed intromission but no ejaculation. Both the mounting and intromission were found to be definitely rewarding but not nearly as strong as when ejaculation was permitted. There was even some evidence that repeated intromission without sexual release was frustrating and tended to produce an avoidance of the female. There are some obvious parallels on the human level.

The events during sexual intercourse have been described by Havelock Ellis as a preparatory stage during which tension builds up, the climax in which tension is released, and a quiescent, peaceful stage called sexual *analepsis*. If orgasm is not reached, tension continues and prevents the sexual analepsis. For example, if a wife does not have an orgasm she may develop hostile feelings toward her husband and find sexual relations aversive. This situation can lead to marital difficulties and divorce in our culture.

Our discussion so far raises the whole question of the nature of sexual reward. It is possible that sexual relations are engaged in for the express purpose of reproduction. This would seem unlikely with animals, but there are instances when it might be true with human beings. Educated people sometimes make a decision to have children and regulate their sexual activity according to medical advice. Nevertheless, this attitude could hardly be the basis for all sexual behavior. For example, the Trobriand Islanders, a primitive people in the southwest Pacific, are ignorant of the connection between sexual activity and reproduction. Yet they have quite elaborate sexual lives, considerably freer than ours.

It would seem more likely that species reproduction is a biological by-product of an activity in which people engage because of a more immediate personal reward. A conspicuous feature of this reward is intense sensory pleasure. In fact, sexual behavior can be taken as one of the best examples for the hedonic theories of motivation. Some features of the pleasure seem to be dependent on drive-reduction, however. As Kagan's studies show, mounting and intromission—which presumably increase tension—are rewarding initially, but may become aversive if tension-release is not forthcoming. This finding suggests that, to some extent, the pleasure of arousal is an anticipation of the tension-release. About all we can say, at the present time, is that both hedonic arousal and drive-reduction are involved in sexual reward.

Sexual Deprivation and Satiation

At one time, a parallel was drawn between homeostatic and sexual motives in that sexual motivation builds up as a function of time after each sexual experience. This time lapse was thought to represent a deprivation period analogous to food deprivation. It was thought that the secretions of the sexual glands accumulate over time and produce a physical tension similar to the tension of eliminative motives. However, this was disproved by the demonstration of a continued sexual motive after the sex glands of males were removed by castration. It is possible that sexual hormone levels decrease after sexual intercourse and build up again over time, but no one has ever been able to demonstrate this condition, and it seems unlikely.

Nevertheless, something like a build-up of sexual motivation over time does occur in male animals and must be explained. The phenomenon is clearly illustrated in a study by Marvin Schwartz. First, he allowed male rats unlimited copulation until they would no longer respond to a receptive female. He then tested their sexual responsiveness after periods of one, three, and six days. The results showed that the number of animals reaching an ejaculation, during a test period, increased over time.

There are two ways of looking at these results. For some psychologists, Schwartz's data simply show that sexual deprivation results in increased sexual activity. Other psychologists view the results as indicating a recovery from sexual fatigue. They point out that no metabolic need is building up and none is fulfilled by the sexual activity. Sexual activity leads to exhaustion from which the animal must recover. It is not a simple matter to distinguish between deprivation and recovery from fatigue.

Frank Beach distinguishes two entirely different mechanisms of sexual arousal and satiation. The first he calls a *general sexual arousal,* which would be largely controlled by the environmental and psychological stimuli we have discussed. The second is a *specific genital arousal.* He bases this distinction on experimental observations of sexual behavior in male rats. The general sexual arousal of the male consists of his attraction to the courting run of the receptive female—a specific darting and stopping, accompanied by a curious wiggling of the ears. The specific genital arousal is that attained by the successive intromissions leading to ejaculation. In the experiments under discussion, it was found that ejaculation had opposite effects on general sexual arousal and genital arousal. With successive ejaculations, the number of intromissions required for the next ejaculation decreased. In other words, ejaculation facilitated genital arousal. On the other hand, successive ejaculations decreased the general sexual arousal provided by the courting run of the female. A longer and longer time elapsed before the female would interest the male again. This shows how complex the whole question of deprivation and satiation in the sexual area really is. Ejaculation has opposite effects on the two mechanisms.

In short, we see that although sex serves no homeostatic need, it does operate as a psychological motive. A sexual reward will motivate learning and performance. Sexual motivation does build up during the time period since the previous sexual experience, but it is not clear if this is a deprivation process analogous to the homeostatic motives or a recovery from fatigue. The situation is further complicated by the opposite effects of sexual intercourse on the two mechanisms of general and genital arousal. It would seem that, although sexual rewards do motivate behavior, they depend on different kinds of arousal and satiation mechanisms than those found in the homeostatic motives.

One of the more startling features of Freud's emphasis on sexual motivation was his insistence that sexuality does not emerge suddenly at puberty but exists from birth and shows a gradual maturation. Although this claim was viewed in some quarters as an attack on childhood innocence, Freud replied that he was merely saying what every nursemaid had known for centuries. There is still considerable controversy over Freud's particular account of sexual maturation, but the mass of scientific evidence gathered during this century supports his main contention.

Sexual Maturation

There is a good deal of evidence that erotic responsiveness is present in some degree from birth and goes through a gradual development. Children have been observed to be genitally responsive during the first year of life, and they may engage in some sort of masturbation. As children develop, their interest in sexual matters and their sexual activity increase. Children are enormously curious about sexual matters and, according to the reports of a large group of mothers, ask many questions, between the ages of two and five, about the different anatomy of the two sexes and the origin of babies. In one study, about half of a group of mothers of preschoolers reported some sort of sex play or genital manipulation. Nursery school children have been found to be interested in viewing others and exhibiting themselves, often to the dismay of their parents.

During the period from age six to twelve, children in some primitive cultures have been observed to engage openly in sex play and masturbation. Little boys and girls play a game of simulated coitus. In these societies, knowledge about sexual matters is given freely by the parents and the children are permitted to observe parental sex relations. The older children in some societies build little huts and play at being married. In general, the sex play of children is partial and immature.

The physiological changes at puberty do usher in a period of heightened sexual interest. According to the Kinsey study, the bulk of the adolescent population in our society engages in masturbation and petting. Transitory homosexual interests may also be aroused at this time. During late adolescence a substantial number engage in premarital intercourse. Although the exact figures given by Kinsey may be inaccurate, there is little doubt that sexual motivation is intense at this time of life and that the cultural code is frequently broken.

For the male, adolescence is the time when sexual desires are at a maximum. There is a gradual decline in sexual motivation from the mid-teens to old age. Women do not show such a marked increase nor do they decline in the same way. There is no marked decline in female sexual motivation even at the time of the menopause, when reproductive capacities are ended.

The development of sexual behavior in monkeys has been studied by Harry F. Harlow, who finds that there are a series of developmental stages— an infantile stage, a pre-adolescent stage, and an adolescent-mature stage. The infantile stage, which in monkeys lasts during the first year of life, consists of immature and inadequate sexual posturing between young monkeys. The male sexual pattern develops first and consists of aggressive threats, immature mounting, and rough-and-tumble play. The female pattern is more passive and also involves grooming the male. The males almost never show the female pattern, but, during the first year, the female sometimes adopts the male posture towards other females.

The pre-adolescent stage begins in the second year and lasts until the third year in females and the fourth in males. It consists of more appropriate and adequate posturing and mounting, but is sexually incomplete. The male pattern continues to be active and the female passive. Masturbation has been frequently observed in male monkeys during this stage but less so in females. Males may also engage in homosexual activity.

The adolescent and adult pattern in monkeys is a continuation of the pre-adolescent behavior, except that now the pattern is complete and impregnation may occur. The male is active and the female passive, but either may initiate sexual relations by assuming the appropriate posture. Male masturbation and homosexual behavior may continue, particularly under conditions of heterosexual deprivation.

Therefore, observations on both human beings and animals suggest that the sexual motive develops gradually from an early age before it blossoms out at puberty. There is some reason to believe that the immature forms of sexual activity—rough-and-tumble play, boys chasing girls on the way to school, necking and petting—play an important part in mature sexual development. Adolescent masturbation and homosexuality appear to be partly due to curiosity and partly serve as substitutive activities. There is no evidence for the old wives' belief that the various forms of childish and adolescent sexual behavior are harmful physically or mentally.

Freud's Psychosexual Stages

Freud's specific account of sexual maturation has not gained the widespread support that his general point has. For one thing, Freud defined sexual phenomena in a very broad way, nearly equating it with sensory pleasure. He felt that there are a number of erotic areas of the body aside from the genitalia—particularly the mouth and anus, but also all the body surface. He assumed that sexual sensitivity, or, in psychoanalytic terms, libidinal energy, is predominant in the region of the mouth for the first year or so of life (the oral stage); then, for about two years, it focuses around the anus (the anal stage); and, subsequently, from about age three to six, it centers in the genitalia (the phallic stage). This is supposed to be followed by a period of sexual inactivity from seven to eleven (the latency stage), which leads to a pre-adolescent interest in members of the same sex (the homosexual stage); finally, mature sexuality ripens during adolescence (the genital stage).

Freud believed that the mature adult's sexual motive contains elements of all the earlier stages of development and is molded by experiences at each of these earlier stages. The major controversy about Freud's theory is not that sexual motivation goes through maturational stages, but that these sexual changes and experiences are the primary basis of adult personality and character. Thus, Freud postulated the oral, anal, and phallic characters, the sublimation of sexual motives in art, religion, and so on. We shall consider this issue in a later chapter. For the moment, we are simply concerned about sexual development per se.

Oral sexuality refers primarily to pleasurable sucking in infants. Freud believed that, in addition to functioning in hunger reduction, sucking is also a source of sensory pleasure and thus, according to his definition, erotic. Extranutritional sucking has been observed frequently in infants, starting shortly after birth and rising to a maximum at about seven months. If sucking pleasure is frustrated in feeding by using a baby bottle with a large hole in the nipple so that little sucking is required to get an adequate amount of food, then extranutritional sucking will increase.

Freud's second stage of psychosexual development, the anal one, reaches its peak around age two. According to Freud the eliminative functions are pleasurable to a child and, again using his broad definition, are therefore sexual. It is true that a child does not have the same abhorrence of these matters that an adult does and may find them interesting and pleasurable. There then ensues a mighty battle between parents and child over toilet training. The child rebels and asserts his independence, but the parents invariably win and the child gives up a source of sexual pleasure.

The phallic stage, according to Freud, marks an increase in interest in the genitalia. Actually, we have seen that masturbatory activity may start at a much earlier age, but it does seem to be true that this becomes more prominent around age three. But the significant thing about the phallic stage is that it is supposed to involve sexual attractions to members of the child's family and produce problems therein. Every society has strong prohibitions against incest.

Freud postulated an undercurrent of sexual attraction and jealousy in families in his famous concept of the Oedipus complex. Oedipus, you will recall, was the king, in the ancient Greek play by Sophocles, who unwittingly killed his father and married his mother. In Freud's theory, as it applies to the male, a little boy develops some sexual feeling for the person who has taken care of all his other needs all during his life—his mother. This feeling becomes intense during the phallic stage from age 3 to 7. However, this incestual feeling puts the boy in a competitive situation with the father. He develops hostile, competitive feelings towards the father but also fears retaliation from this rival. Specifically, his fear is that of being castrated— castration anxiety. Normally, the boy is supposed to resolve his Oedipus complex by renouncing the sexual component in his feelings toward his mother, identifying with his father, and, eventually, becoming the head of his own family.

A situation comparable to the male Oedipus complex is assumed in the case of a little girl. She develops sexual feelings toward her father and competes with her mother. Two things complicate the situation in the case of the little girl. First, as with the boy, her first object of affection is the mother, but, unlike the boy, she has to shift her positive feelings to another person, the father. Second, in discovering the anatomical differences between the sexes, the little girl may come to have a special kind of castration anxiety, a feeling that she has already been castrated. This may develop into a motive known as penis envy, in which she actively competes with boys in masculine pursuits. The girl normally resolves all this by repressing sexual feeling towards her father, identifying with her mother, and having a baby of her own with her own husband.

Following the period of sexual latency—from about age seven to eleven—when sexual activity is supposed to be quiescent, Freud postulated a stage of psychosexual development involving an attraction to members of the same sex. Homosexual behavior has been observed in prepubescent chimpanzees and other primates, mostly in the male but occasionally in the female. So, too, on the human level a number of individuals begin sexual contacts with a member of the same sex during prepubescence or early adolescence.

During adolescence and adulthood, Freud believed, the various forms of childhood sexuality are integrated and subordinated to mature sexuality. The end result is what Freud called the genital stage, in which adult heterosexuality is established in the context of a loving relationship involving mutual respect. It is interesting to see that, although Freud is often cast into the role of a sexual revolutionary, his highest stage of development is the mature, stable kind of marital relationship valued by nearly all societies.

Cultural Factors in Psychosexual Development

A number of theorists and investigators have taken issue with Freud's theory of psychosexual development. One of the main criticisms is that Freud included too much under the term "sexual." Another is that Freud assumed that the various stages unfold on an inner, biological timetable with relatively little influence by the environment. The critics point out that Freud did not take cultural learning into account. Recall that the physiological evidence suggests that human sexuality is largely controlled by cultural factors.

To begin with, what Freud called the oral stage is really far more complex than the concept of oral pleasure would suggest. As we shall see in a later chapter, the first year of life is extremely important in the development of affectional bonds. Sucking is only one part of a complex pattern that includes clinging, rocking, and other nonoral behavior. In addition, the extranutritional sucking, which some take as proof of oral pleasure, has been shown to be largely learned by associating sucking with feeding. Modern psychoanalysts, like Erik H. Erikson, have pointed out that this first period of life is a child's introduction to social relationships, the critical learning being that of basically trusting or not trusting another human being. Although it may have relevance to later sexual relationships, oral pleasure seems secondary to the formation of a social relationship with the mother.

A similar problem has been raised about Freud's anal stage—is the interest a child shows about toilet matters sexual in any meaningful sense? It is now generally agreed by developmental psychologists that toilet training is simply one aspect of the general socialization of a child at this age. Many other aspects of his behavior also come under social control—getting dressed, going to bed on time, inhibiting aggression towards siblings, and so on. The child may rebel against this limitation of his pleasure-seeking behavior, and the main battlefield may or may not be in toilet training.

The most important of Freud's psychosexual concepts is the Oedipus complex. In the case of the boy, fear of the father is said to be an outgrowth of sexual jealousy about the mother. The anthropologist B. K. Malinowski specifically tested the universality of the Oedipus complex in a study of the primitive Trobriand Islanders. He found little hostility on the part of the Trobriand boy towards his father but a great deal toward the brother of the boy's mother. As it turned out, the boy's uncle was given primary responsibility in the boy's discipline, education, and inheritance, while the father played the role of an amiable companion. In this case, sexual jealousy cannot account for the hostility towards authority. In Freud's Victorian Vienna, of course, the father was both the stern disciplinarian and the rival for the mother. On the basis of Malinowski's work, it would seem that the father's disciplinary role provokes most of the hostility in the boy.

It is generally conceded that Freud was describing something of great significance in the idea of the Oedipus complex. Instead of its being an inborn part of the maturing sexual motive, however, it may refer to a common family situation in which jealousy about affection, concern about dominance, and other factors are as important as incestual feelings. The particular form the Oedipus complex takes depends more on the personality of the parents and their interaction than on the biological maturation of the child.

Freud's view of the female Oedipus complex, with emphasis on penis envy, has been seriously challenged by members of the cultural school of psychoanalysis. These modern psychoanalysts, while agreeing with Freud on the importance of family relationships, believe that Freud viewed sexual matters in too narrow and biological a fashion. These matters gain meaning through the cultural values attached to them, they say. Thus, in the case of penis envy in the girl, they believe that the basic jealousy is not over the specific features of the male anatomy but over the advantageous social role and the freedom accorded males in our culture. In many groups, male children are more highly prized than females. The jealousy stemming from this preference may be symbolized in dreams and fantasies by penis envy, but the basic motive is a desire for social equality.

The gradual and continuous development of sexual behavior among people in permissive cultures and among primates stands in sharp contrast to the Freudian concept of a latency period in the human being from about age seven to eleven during which no overt sexual behavior is supposed to appear. Observations of cultures around the world indicate that there is no universal latency period—in many cultures sexual play is uninterrupted from infancy to adolescence. Nevertheless, Freud's observations of his own Viennese culture were probably correct and could be extended to our own society. Even so, it would seem that this is a result of cultural inhibition rather than of a biological lapse in maturation.

Adult sexual behavior and marital adjustment are also strongly conditioned by cultural attitudes about sexuality. In the Victorian era, sexual motivation was strongly inhibited. In Polynesia, the attitudes are free and easy. In our society today, there is much confusion, uncertainty, and ambivalence. These cultural attitudes are reflected in problems of sexual development and in problems of sexual adjustment in marriage. It is important, also, to keep in mind that marital relations are simply one part of a complex human relationship. Many of the problems of marital adjustment concerning emotional security, dominance and submission, dependence and independence, and career ambitions are fought out on the sexual battleground. Since sexual relations are such an intimate matter, our deepest feelings about ourselves become involved—our sense of adequacy, our willingness to be close to another human being, and our ability to face maturity.

Emotional Motives

Imagine a man who is driving along a road when another car suddenly darts out of a driveway. The man is frightened, he feels a sinking sensation in the pit of his stomach, and his muscles tense up. The effect on his behavior is dramatic—he jams his foot down hard on the brake pedal and rapidly turns the steering wheel. There is a screeching of the brakes followed by the sickening sound of breaking glass and crumpling of fenders. The man sits for a moment and then the fear turns to anger—this idiot has frightened him, upset his schedule, and caused damage to his car. The anger also has dramatic effects on his behavior—he sets

48

5

his jaw and strides toward the other car. Then, he sees that the other driver is injured, with blood streaming down his face. The man has a wave of nausea, a twinge of guilt, and a strong feeling of compassion. Once more behavior is mobilized—the man administers first aid and calls for an ambulance.

We are talking here about emotions—powerful reactions that have motivating effects on behavior. Emotions are physiological and psychological responses that influence perception, learning, and performance. The area of emotion is complicated by the lack of general agreement on a basic definition of the nature of the concept. For example, some people take the position that emotion is an entirely different process from motivation. Others say that emotions are simply one class of motives. Some define emotion subjectively— in terms of the feelings experienced by the individual. Others see emotions as bodily changes. Most of these people have emphasized the *reaction* as the main component in emotion, but others concentrate on the *perception* of the situation that arouses the emotion or the *effects* of the emotion on ordinary behavior. In philosophical thought up until the nineteenth century, the problem of the relation of consciously experienced emotions and bodily changes was relatively simple: We consciously experience an emotion and the bodily changes follow from that.

The first person to seriously challenge the classical position was William James, the famous Harvard psychologist. In 1884, he wrote that conscious experience follows the bodily reactions, which are more or less automatic reactions to stimuli in the environment. The most important part of the bodily reaction is in the internal visceral organs—the heart, stomach, blood vessels, and so on. Thus, the sight of a bear causes an internal upset that is subsequently perceived as fear. Instead of the classical interpretation, which would be something like "I see the bear, I feel afraid, my body prepares to run away," James put the sequence as "I see the bear, my body prepares to run away, I feel afraid." Of course, James realized that learning is involved in determining which stimuli will evoke the visceral responses, but the *feeling* comes not from the perception of a dangerous stimulus but from the visceral responses that follow. Since a Danish scientist, Carl Lange, put forth a similar theory at about the same time, the basic notion has come to be known as the James-Lange theory of emotions.

Almost from its inception, the James-Lange theory has been subject to criticism. Walter Cannon, for example, summarized evidence showing that experimental animals and patients who have had the neural connections severed between the viscera and the brain still show rage, fear, and other emotional reactions.

Another approach to this problem is to produce the visceral changes associated with emotion, independent of external stimuli, and see whether a subject experiences the emotion. This goal can be achieved by injecting a subject with certain chemical substances that produce bodily changes. For example, adrenalin will increase heart rate and change other bodily processes. The James-Lange theory would have to predict that the subjects would experience emotion along with these bodily changes. Yet subjects do not experience a true emotion—they report that they feel "as if" they were afraid or "as if" they were anticipating a joyous event.

On the other hand, drugs acting on the viscera do affect the reaction of the subject to external stimuli. In one study, by Stanley Schachter and his associates, subjects were injected with either adrenalin, a tranquilizer, or a control solution of saline which has no visceral effects. They were then shown a slapstick movie. Those subjects with adrenalin were highly amused, those with saline next, while those with the tranquilizer were least amused. These experiments suggest that visceral responses are important in predisposing a subject to react to an emotional stimulus but that they are not sufficient, by themselves, to produce the full emotion.

Walter Cannon, one of the chief critics of the James-Lange theory, proposed an alternative explanation of emotion and bodily change. This is the "thalamic" theory of emotion, which was also suggested by P. Bard and has become known as the Cannon-Bard theory. According to this theory, incoming sensory impulses pass through the thalamus, which is at the base of the brain near the hypothalamus. During the transit in the thalamus, according to the Cannon-Bard idea, the incoming messages receive an "emotional quale." Ordinarily, the cortex inhibits this emotional reaction in the thalamus but, if it does not, then emotion is released. This consists of a simultaneous discharge of the thalamus upwards to the cortex—which constitutes the conscious emotional experience—and downwards to the body—which produces the visceral and muscular expression. As we shall see later, the Cannon-Bard theory—oversimplified as it was—is close to current neurophysiological thinking about emotions and the importance of brain mechanisms.

Although there is no definitive solution to the question of the relationship between emotional experience and bodily expression, a most sensible hypothesis has been put forth by Magda Arnold. First of all, she says that most of the emphasis has been on the second half of the sequence—emotion, expression, action—and not enough on the initial perception. She also points out that not every perception leads to an emotional reaction, so that there has to be some mechanism for appraising the situation. She suggests the following sequence:

1. Perception—the neutral reception of external stimuli (for example, a bomber pilot sees a fighter plane approaching him).
2. Appraisal—a judgment of the stimuli as good and beneficial or bad and harmful (the pilot recognizes the plane as an enemy who could shoot him down).
3. Emotion—a felt tendency towards stimuli judged as good and away from those judged as bad (the pilot has a tendency to flee).
4. Expression—a pattern of physiological changes organized towards approach or withdrawal, differing for each emotion, which *accompanies* the felt tendency (the pilot's heart pounds, his muscles tense, his mouth becomes dry, he breaks out in a cold sweat, and he has butterflies in his stomach).
5. Action—approach or withdrawal may occur if another emotion does not interfere (the pilot may not actually flee because of a sense of duty, a desire for glory, and so on).

An important feature of Arnold's theory is that emotion is defined in a motivational sense. The tendency to approach or withdraw is a basic form of the directional aspect of a motive, while the visceral changes are seen as preparations for the body to carry out the behavior. This is very close to McDougall's theory, mentioned in Chapter 1, in which each motive is thought to be accompanied by a characteristic emotion.

In this chapter, we shall take the position that emotions are a special class of motives. Although internal predisposing conditions, such as homeostatic imbalance, are important in motives like hunger, emotions are to a much greater extent aroused by external stimuli—learned and unlearned. So, too, the bodily changes in emotion are more dramatic than in other motivational states. However, this sequence is motivational because of its eventual effects on behavior. Thus, an emotion is an externally aroused motive with important bodily accompaniments.

The plan of this chapter is to follow roughly Arnold's outline of the emotional sequence. First, we shall discuss emotional arousal, which will cover what Arnold calls perception and appraisal. Then we shall discuss the emotional reaction itself—the conscious experience, the bodily changes, and the brain mechanisms involved. Finally, we shall examine the effects of emotion on behavior, with particular reference to a comparison of emotion and motivation. During this presentation we shall mention a great many emotions briefly, but two will serve as the major examples—fear and anger. This is not because they are more important than other emotions but because more is known about them.

THE AROUSAL OF EMOTION

Emotions are aroused by a variety of innate stimulus patterns, learned stimuli, and social situations. Generally speaking, the importance of learning and social facilitation increases as we go up the evolutionary scale—the appraisal part of the process is more important, in Arnold's terms. Thus, certain types of protozoa automatically swim away from strong sunlight, whereas a man may be made fearful by the passing thought that life is, after all, quite meaningless. We shall consider innate stimuli, learning, and personal threat in emotional arousal.

Innate Emotional Arousal

The emotion of fear can be produced in an animal, a child, or an adult by nearly any sudden and intense stimulus. In laboratory experiments, the pain produced by electrical stimulation is frequently used to elicit fear. John Watson found that from birth on, a child shows fear whenever a sudden loud noise is made nearby. Jerking away a child's blanket or suddenly dropping a child a short distance also produces fear. It is the unexpected nature of the stimulus, as well as its intensity, that produces fear.

The stimuli that elicit fear increase in number and complexity as we go up the evolutionary scale. Donald Hebb gives the following examples: A rat is made fearful by pain, sudden loud noise, sudden loss of support, and strange surroundings. A dog is also made fearful by these things but, in addition, may be frightened by a balloon being blown up, its master in unusual clothing, or a strange person. Monkeys and apes are made fearful by an enormous list of things—a carrot of unusual shape, a biscuit with a worm in it, a doll, and so on. Nearly all adult chimpanzees are terrified by a life-size clay model of a chimpanzee head—some scream and run out of sight. Strangeness seems to be the key factor.

Now Hebb points out that, although these fears are not learned in the usual sense, they do require some learning as a background. For example, around four months of age chimpanzee infants show an intense fear of strangers, and human infants show the same thing at around six to eight months of age. By this time they have learned which adults are familiar so that a new and totally unfamiliar adult is perceived as strange.

Anger is another emotion that may be produced by certain situations on an innate basis. Angry feelings are very often associated with aggression—temper tantrums, fighting, verbal attacks. As we shall see later, however, the two are not identical and may occur independently. Nevertheless, angry aggression is commonly observed in a great many species as a reaction to certain situations.

According to some theorists—notably Sigmund Freud—aggression is an instinct constantly seeking an outlet in destructiveness, war, and sadism. In this depressing view, social life is inevitably full of hate and hostility. The best we can hope for, in civilization, is to find harmless outlets for this innate aggression—prize fights, business competition, or political power struggles.

One has only to think of the history of mankind to be convinced of the prevalence of aggressive and destructive behavior. However, the mere prevalence of a form of behavior is no proof that it is instinctive, in the sense of a tendency constantly seeking discharge. Angry aggression may be an instinctive reaction to certain situations, but it is aroused only when the situations present themselves.

Observations of lower animals show that they fight only under certain circumstances—to escape being captured, to avoid pain, for possession of females, in defense of their young, for territorial hunting rights, and to protect a privileged position of dominance in their group. In other words, fighting is not something that constantly seeks an outlet but a response that may occur when an animal is threatened, angered, or blocked in obtaining certain goals.

In 1939, a group of Yale psychologists formulated the frustration-aggression hypothesis that seems to be particularly pertinent to the angry kind of aggression under discussion. Frustration was defined as the blocking of a motivated, goal-directed sequence of behavior. An example is the child who hears the bell of an ice-cream vendor and implores his mother to buy him some. When the mother decides it is too close to dinnertime and refuses, the child is frustrated and may feel angry and become aggressive towards the mother. According to the hypothesis, frustration frequently produces angry aggression, and, conversely, the angry, emotional sort of aggression is often traceable to frustration.

As we have seen, an infant
is made fearful, initially, by relatively few stimuli. Yet, as he grows up, he
may be afraid of more and more things. The fears of adults are even more
varied and idiosyncratic. To some extent, these changes are due to maturation.
Nevertheless, a large part of the introduction of new fears and the elimination
of old ones depends on learning.

The simplest form of learning is the *conditioning* process. The basic principle is that a previously neutral stimulus will, when paired with a stimulus
that innately arouses a response, become *conditioned* and arouse the response
itself. For example, a mild tone does not ordinarily arouse fear in a laboratory
animal. Suppose however, that the tone is sounded and then followed by an
electric shock that does arouse fear. Suppose further that the tone and shock
are paired this way several times. Now when the tone is sounded by itself,
the animal will show fear.

The learning of a simple fear was demonstrated some years ago by John
Watson. Most children are unafraid of mice, rats, snakes, and other animals
that many adults find loathsome. Albert, an eleven-month-old child, showed
no fear of a white rat, but he was afraid of a loud sound made by striking a
bar. Each time Albert touched the white rat, the bar was struck. After seven
combinations of loud sound and white rat, Albert had become quite frightened of the animal.

Fears may also be extended to other, similar stimuli by the process of
generalization. For example, a laboratory animal that has become afraid of
a tone may show fear of somewhat different tones, even though fear had never
been directly conditioned to them. Watson showed that Albert's fear of the
white rat generalized to similar objects like a white rabbit, cotton wool, and a
fur coat. It did not generalize to the child's wooden blocks and other objects
dissimilar to the white rat.

Fears may be eliminated by the process of *extinction*. This consists of
repeatedly presenting a tone, or other previously neutral stimulus, without a
shock. Eventually, fear is no longer produced by the tone. Extinction cannot be achieved too abruptly, however. Throwing a fearful person into a
swimming pool may only increase his fears. Fears are better eliminated by
gradually exposing a person to the fearful stimulus and *replacing* the fear
response with something more relaxing. For example, in eliminating the fear
of a child to a rabbit, Mary Cover Jones presented the rabbit to the child at
the other end of the room while the child was eating. Eating is somewhat
incompatible with fear and may replace it. Eventually, she was able to bring
the rabbit closer without the arousal of fear. Finally, she could dispense with
the eating.

Most children's fears are, however, probably learned in a more complex
way. Many children are afraid of things with which they have had no direct
experience. This may be based on *imitation* of the parent's fears. One study
showed that children tend to have the same fears as their mothers. This was
especially true of fears of dogs, insects, and storms.

The stimuli that arouse anger may also be learned, but this area has not
been studied extensively. It is clear that a child may respond with anger not

Emotional
Motives

only to a physical blocking of his wish to go outdoors, say, but also to his mother's simply saying "No." The reaction to the verbal prohibition is probably learned by some sort of conditioning procedure. The mother follows "No" by pulling the child back inside and locking the door. People grow up learning that different sorts of cues lead to frustration. For some people, anything short of an enthusiastic "Yes" to a request amounts to a signal for frustration—they have heard too many "Maybe's" in their lifetime.

Personal Threat

The innate physical stimuli and the cues associated with them account for only a part of the situations that arouse emotions in human beings. Emotions are also aroused by threats to our more personal and social motives. These motives will be discussed in later chapters, but for the moment we can say that they revolve around our self-esteem and the social goals that are important to us in a personal sense.

Psychoanalytic theorists point to this source of emotional arousal when they distinguish between *fear* and *anxiety*. Now, physiologically these two are identical—both involve a palpitating heart and a feeling of dread. Fear, however, is usually thought to involve a specific, physical threat whereas anxiety is a more general reaction to personal threats. Ask yourself what would make you anxious in a personal sense—doubt thrown on your intelligence, honesty, or sexuality; an attack on your moral or religious values; a shaking of your faith in your friends and loved ones; or an undermining of your belief in yourself as a worthwhile human being? People are threatened by different things, but for each of us there are some threats that arouse anxiety.

This was demonstrated experimentally by W. Vogel, S. Raymond, and R. S. Lazarus. Two groups of high school students were studied—one showed evidence of being strongly motivated toward academic achievement and the other toward friendship and sociability. They were then presented with situations that threatened either their achievement strivings or their social acceptability. The former group showed their largest physiological stress reaction when achievement was threatened, while the other group reacted physiologically to a greater extent when their social acceptability was threatened. The emotional arousal depended on a threat to something of personal importance.

It is clear from the above experiment that the reaction to a threatening situation depends on some sort of personal evaluation of the nature of the threat. This brings us back to Arnold's *appraisal* of the stimulus in the arousal of emotion. The importance of this appraisal was demonstrated in an experiment by J. C. Speisman, R. S. Lazarus, A. Mordkoff, and L. Davison. These investigators used a particularly strong emotional stimulus—a movie showing the puberty ceremonies of the Arunta, a primitive Australian tribe. The ceremony includes a subincision operation—the boy is held down by several naked men and a crude incision is made along the underside of the penis with a stone knife, with no anesthesia and under unsanitary conditions. Several studies have shown that this movie arouses rather powerful emotions.

The purpose of Speisman and his associates was to try to influence the emotional reaction by altering the appraisal of the situation. This was done by using several accompanying sound tracks with different content. One group saw the movie with a sound track that emphasized *intellectualization*—that is, the whole procedure was described in a detached, unemotional way, as an anthropologist would view any interesting primitive custom. The second group had a sound track which emphasized *denial* and *reaction formation*—it was said that the operation was not painful and that the native boys found the occasion a joyful one. A third group had a *trauma* track in which the painful aspects were highlighted, and the last group saw the movie without a sound track. The results showed that, at the emotional peak of the film, the actual operation, the groups differed in their physiological response. The trauma track group reacted the most, the silent film group next, and the two defensive groups (intellectualization, and denial-reaction formation) least.

Psychotherapy is used to help neurotic and psychotic individuals. We are just beginning to understand psychotherapy, but recent research indicates that it works best with personally threatened people and involves a reduction in anxiety, enabling a person to think more clearly and solve his problems more adaptively. One important process here is analogous to extinction—the person talks about forbidden things in the permissive atmosphere of the therapy.

Personal threat may also take the form of a frustration of individual or group striving toward a goal and therefore produce anger and aggression. There is evidence that a large part of the angry aggression in social life—crime, revolution, racial violence, and so on—is related to economic, social, and personal frustrations. Frustration may be one of the factors leading to war. The rise of Hitler and the consequent bloodshed has been related to the humiliating terms of the peace treaty after World War I as well as to the economic frustrations produced by inflation and depression in Germany during the twenties and thirties. This explanation is largely theoretical because it is difficult to study complex phenomena like war. But intergroup hostilities, on a smaller scale, have been studied experimentally.

Muzafer and Carolyn Sherif studied group conflict in an experimental camp for twelve-year-old boys. The boys were divided into two groups of twelve each and housed separately. After a time each group developed cohesion and leadership, with a friendly rivalry between them. The two groups were then brought together for athletic competition in such a way that one group consistently lost. Other planned frustrations were also introduced. The result was bitter hostility between the two groups, including a near riot in the mess hall, raids on one another's campsite, and talk of "war." The group frustration, involving loss of esteem, appeared to be the critical factor.

The Sherifs also tried to reduce the intergroup hostility. Combining forces to play an outside team helped, but this just meant larger-scale hostilities to other groups. Working together on projects was the most promising method tried. Many psychologists, today, are deeply concerned with alleviating international tensions and preventing nuclear war. Their suggestions have included increased international understanding and cooperation, gradually reducing armaments while inviting other countries to do the same, and reducing the economic and social frustrations in underdeveloped countries that would predispose the inhabitants to aggression.

In summary, emotional reactions can be aroused innately by a number of situations—for example, fear by a loud noise and anger by frustration. New sources of fear and anger can be learned by conditioning or imitation and extended to similar situations by generalization. Old fears and anxieties may be eliminated by extinction. On the human level, an important source of emotional arousal is personal threat—a disturbance of self-esteem or an interference with social motivation. Personal threat depends, to a large extent, on the individual's appraisal of the situation and how it relates to his own social motives.

Once an emotion is aroused by an external stimulus, what happens in a person? As we saw earlier, there are changes in the person's subjective experience and in his body. In this section we shall first attempt to describe and classify the various kinds of emotional reaction, largely based on subjective reports or general observations. Then, we shall describe the bodily changes—first the overt behavioral patterns and then the internal physiological events. Finally, we shall try to tie all these changes together by considering the brain mechanisms involved in all aspects of emotional reaction.

Classification of Emotions

The list of feelings and reactions we include under the term emotion is almost infinite. A few that come to mind readily are: fear, anger, rage, horror, terror, agony, anxiety, jealousy, shame, embarrassment, disgust, grief, boredom, and dejection. These tend to be the negative emotions, but positive ones can be added: love, joy, amusement, elation, ecstasy, pleasure, and happiness. It is quite clear that the list could be extended indefinitely, depending only on one's introspective skill and vocabulary range.

The scientific task is to see if there is any order in the endless expanse of emotional experience. Is it possible that, at birth, there are just a few basic emotional reactions that develop and combine in various ways, through learning and maturation, to cover the full spectrum of emotional experience as we know it as adults? The behaviorist, John Watson, thought so and postulated three basic emotions in children—fear, rage, and love. Subsequent studies have shown, however, that emotional reactivity at birth is even simpler than Watson believed.

Observations of children in a foundling home, ranging in age from birth to two years, showed that initially an infant is either excited or quiescent. Stimuli of any kind elicit only the generalized excitement pattern. However, as shown in Figure 5, the general excitement becomes differentiated as the infant develops.

Do these emotional reactions continue to be differentiated through the life span to account for the myriad of adult emotions? It would appear that repeated subdivision could not account for the kind of mixed feelings many adults have. For example, the feeling of guilt may be a combination of joy and fear—the forbidden pleasure. A fusion of quite distinct emotions appears to be involved here rather than a simple differentiation.

Robert Plutchik has proposed a theory of emotional mixture. He assumes

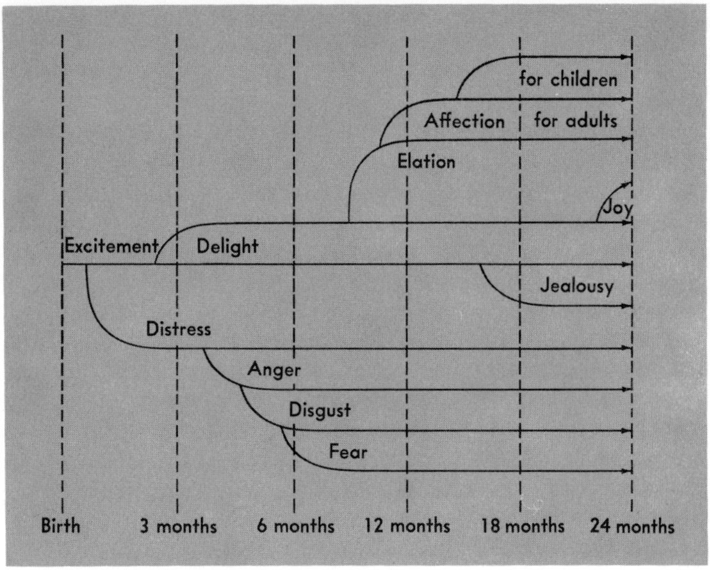

Figure 5. Differentiation of emotions during early development. Observations of infants and young children show that specific emotions are formed by a differentiation of more generalized reactions. (After K. Bridges. Emotional development in early infancy. Child Dev., 1932, 3, 324–341.)

that there are eight basic emotional reactions—anticipation, anger, joy, acceptance, surprise, fear, sorrow, and disgust. These are patterned bodily reactions for which we can find prototypes in lower animals. They have shown changes in evolution and probably require maturation in the individual. The complex emotional experience in human adults is attained by a mixture of these eight basic reactions, according to Plutchik.

Plutchik also assumes that each primary emotional reaction can vary in intensity, producing different shades of emotional experience. Judgments of the words we use to describe emotional experience indicate that a basic reaction like fear can vary in intensity from timidity, through apprehension, fear, and panic, up to terror. So, too, we have annoyance, anger, and rage as well as calmness, serenity, pleasure, happiness, joy, and ecstasy. Combinations of different emotions at different levels of intensity could further explain the rich variety of emotional experience. For instance, a mixture of intense joy and mild fear could account for the guilt-tinged happiness we may feel when on a big shopping spree.

A final evaluation of Plutchik's theory, or a similar one, must await information about the evolution of the prototypical reactions and brain mechanisms for them. Other psychologists have preferred to take a more descriptive approach to the classification of emotions. The descriptive approach involves the isolation of one or more basic *dimensions* along which emotional reactions can be placed. Three main dimensions have been described by various authors: intensity, pleasantness-unpleasantness, and approach-avoidance.

The intensity dimension is the one most psychologists have agreed upon. This has also been called level of arousal or activation. Donald Lindsley, basing his conception on physiological data, believes that most behavior can be described along a continuum of activation ranging from death, through coma, deep sleep, light sleep, drowsiness, relaxed wakefulness, and alert attentiveness, to excited emotion. Elizabeth Duffy has suggested that the term emotion be replaced by arousal or energy mobilization. Others have gone so far as to suggest that the only real difference between any of the emotions is in level of arousal.

There is, nevertheless, good evidence that emotions are differentiated along dimensions other than intensity. Emotions at the same level of intensity may be pleasant or unpleasant. Thus, terror and ecstasy may be equally arousing but quite easily distinguished. A number of studies have shown that pleasantness-unpleasantness, or some synonym of this dimension, is a factor independent of level of arousal. Among the more aroused emotions appear joy, astonishment, hopefulness, and ecstasy on the pleasant side and disgust, fear, rage, and terror on the unpleasant. Among the less aroused emotions there are the pleasantness of maternal feeling and the unpleasantness of grief.

The dimension of approach-avoidance is equivalent to the definition by Arnold of an emotional experience as a felt tendency towards some stimuli or a felt tendency away from others. In many cases, the approach tendency is towards stimuli that arouse pleasant feelings and the avoidance one away from those associated with unpleasant ones. This is not always the case, however, so the approach-avoidance dimension is evidently different from the pleasantness-unpleasantness one. For example, anger is unpleasant but it may involve an approach towards the object for purposes of attack. Contempt is an emotion that has pleasant features but is usually accompanied by an avoidance tendency.

In general, the bewildering variety of emotions can be classified according to several principles. The generalized emotional reaction at birth is *differentiated* during development. On the adult level, we can distinguish a few basic emotions which *combine* in various ways to produce subtle emotions. Finally, emotional experience can be described in terms of several *dimensions,* such as level of intensity, pleasantness-unpleasantness, and approach-avoidance.

Overt Bodily Patterns

Nearly a hundred years ago, Charles Darwin wrote the first important scientific book about emotion. He argued that emotional patterns are really inherited reactions which have had *biological utility* in the evolution of the species. He concentrated on the observable muscular patterns—bodily movements and postures. Thus, the baring of the teeth, bristling and growling, which we associate with hostility in animals, are really ways of preparing for attack and defense. In man, this survives as the sneer and gritting of the teeth when he feels hostile.

Other emotional patterns appear to be the opposite of hostility. Thus, the expression of friendliness tends to reverse the behavior of hostility. This fits Darwin's principle of *antithesis*. The muscular rigidity, bristling hair, and growling of the hostile dog are replaced by a fluid relaxation, a wagging tail, a smoothing of the hair, and an ingratiating whine. Apparently, this communicates a lack of threat and permits social contact.

On the human level, we often recognize the emotional tone of an individual by his movements and posture. We suspect that a rigid or fidgety person is tense. Large assertive movements may suggest hostility. Relaxation and graceful movements make us think of a positive feeling. For human beings, the most important overt muscular expression of emotion occurs in the face. We read the faces of people to assess their feelings more than we observe their gross behavior. The accuracy of such a reading has had a long history of controversy in psychology. Early studies threw a great deal of doubt on whether people could accurately judge emotion on the basis of facial expression. The current evidence suggests that, although a precise discrimination among facial expressions of similar emotions is difficult, people are able to distinguish major patterns.

In a recent study, H. Schlosberg had subjects look at photographs of models posing with different expressions and rate them along two dimensions—pleasant-unpleasant and attention-rejection (attention-rejection is Schlosberg's equivalent of approach-avoidance). There was good agreement on the ratings. The pictures high on both the pleasant and attention dimension suggest emotions like happiness. Unpleasant and attentive pictures suggest an interested anger. The pictures rated as pleasant but rejecting suggest contempt, and those unpleasant and rejecting disgust. Later Schlosberg obtained evidence for a third dimension in these facial expressions—level of activation, or intensity.

To what extent are facial expressions innately related to emotion, and to what extent are they learned? Children who are deaf and blind tend to show the same expressions, in the same situations, at about the same age as normal children. This suggests innate patterns. At the same time, social learning has some effect on the way emotions are expressed facially. Americans usually express surprise by raising the eyebrows but the Chinese stick out their tongues.

In summary, emotions may be expressed in gross bodily movements and facial expressions. Facial expressions can be described in terms of dimensions like intensity and pleasantness-unpleasantness which correspond to the dimensions describing subjective emotional experience. Although these patterns are clearly inherited in lower animals, the human reactions also show the influence of social learning.

Internal Physiological Changes

It is clear to anyone who has experienced an emotion that the most significant bodily changes are internal. Are the racing heart and the sinking feeling in the pit of the stomach merely signs of internal disorganization? No, they appear to be meaningful bodily processes. Walter Cannon extended Darwin's idea of emotional expression as serviceable habits to the internal responses. He suggested that the internal changes represented an *emergency reaction* that prepares the body for *fight* or *flight*.

The action of the internal visceral organs (the heart, lungs, stomach, intestines, and so on) is under the control of the autonomic nervous system. This system has two main divisions—the parasympathetic and the sympathetic—which operate in somewhat opposite directions. The parasympathetic system is mainly concerned with the vegetative or housekeeping functions of the body. It stimulates the secretion of saliva and digestive fluids, the peristaltic movements of the gastrointestinal tract, and digestion in general. The parasympathetic system acts to slow down breathing and heart rate and to aid the flow of blood to the intestines.

The sympathetic nervous system swings into action when some emergency faces the individual. The changes in bodily function can be thought of as preparing for exertion. The digestive process is slowed down and the blood flow shunted to the brain and muscles where it will be needed. The heart beats more rapidly to supply these organs more quickly. Breathing quickens to supply more oxygen and the liver releases a ready supply of sugar for energy. Other changes, of some remote adaptive function, occur, such as the opening of the iris of the eye, the erection of hairs, and the increase in sweating. According to Cannon, the body is now prepared for *fight* or *flight*.

Along with the sympathetic nervous system, the glandular endocrine system plays a major role in this alarm reaction. This system is controlled by the pituitary gland, but the mode of action involves several hormones secreted by the adrenal glands. Adrenal hormones have effects on circulation, salt retention, the production of sugar, and the control of inflammation. This whole stress reaction can be set into motion by hundreds of damaging physical stimuli and also by emotional stimuli.

The reaction to stress also depends on whether the stress is acute or chronic. The initial reaction to stress is described by Hans Selye as the *stage of alarm,* during which the bodily changes are consistent with an idea of an emergency reaction. If the stress is prolonged, however, the reaction enters a *stage of resistance.* The body compensates for the stress and, in a manner of speaking, tries to live with it. During this stage of resistance the body is quite vulnerable and a second stress may catapult it into a final, terminal period known as the *stage of exhaustion.*

An important aspect of Cannon's emergency theory is that the bodily reactions in a variety of emotional states—including pain, hunger, fear, and rage—are essentially the same. This theory has been extended by some psychologists to all emotional states—the only thing that differentiates emotions is the level of general arousal. This idea may have been influenced by the heavy emphasis on the negative, excited emotions. The bodily reactions in the maternal feeling during nursing an infant at the breast must surely be different. However, even with the negative, excited emotions, there is evidence of a differential bodily reaction.

The emotions of anger and fear represent the fight or flight alternatives suggested by Cannon. During his time they seemed similar in bodily reaction and seemed to be under the control of the adrenal hormone called *adrenalin.* Recent research, however, has shown that there are at least *two* adrenal hormones important in emotion—*adrenalin* and *noradrenalin.* They have somewhat different effects on the body and appear to be related to different emotions. Adrenalin is most closely associated with fear and noradrenalin with anger. For example, peaceful and easily frightened animals, like rabbits, secrete mostly adrenalin, whereas animals who exist by attacking, like lions, have a preponderance of noradrenalin.

Daniel Funkenstein has shown that college students in a frustrating task react in three ways: Some showed fear, some expressed anger outwards at the experimenters, and others showed a depressive reaction which consisted of expressing anger at themselves or, in other words, blaming themselves. The students expressing anger outwards showed a physiological reaction suggesting that the hormone noradrenalin was being secreted. An adrenalin reaction was shown by the students with a fearful or depressive reaction.

We can say, then, that emotion involves an internal physiological reaction mediated by the sympathetic nervous system and the endocrines. Acute stress consists of an emergency reaction preparing the body for fight or flight. Chronic stress produces a resistance stage that may lead to psychosomatic disease. Although some people maintain that the internal changes are the same in all emotions, there is evidence that for at least some emotions—for instance, fear and anger—the changes are different.

Brain Mechanisms in Emotion

The Cannon-Bard thalamic theory of emotion is oversimplified, but it did open up the possibility that emotions are complex behavioral patterns controlled by mechanisms in the brain. Much of the recent work on the physiology of emotion has concentrated on these central controlling mechanisms rather than the muscular or autonomic changes.

There are two general systems in the brain that are thought to be involved in emotion. The first is called the limbic system. This includes parts of the thalamus and hypothalamus, and also certain adjacent parts of the cortex—the inner core of the cortex, not the outer part. This inner core evolved earlier than the outer part, and it is essentially the same in man, monkeys, and lower mammals, whereas the outer part has shown the dramatic evolutionary changes. For this reason, the inner core is thought to be the archaic, primitive brain and is called the paleocortex (old cortex), while the outer part is the neocortex (new cortex). These brain areas are shown in Figure 6.

As we saw earlier, it is the limbic system that is involved in many of the homeostatic motives and contains the pleasure and pain areas. It is also closely related to the autonomic reactions and bodily changes associated with emotion. Stimulation of various parts of the limbic system produces fear, rage, and other emotional reactions.

The reactions to stimulation of the limbic system can be conditioned and have the motivating effect that naturally aroused emotions do. J. M. R. Delgado, W. W. Roberts, and N. E. Miller aroused fear in cats by electrical stimulation of the limbic system. After pairing a tone with the brain stimulation, they were able to arouse fear by the tone alone. Then they were able to show that the cats would learn to rotate a wheel to turn off the tone. This is the way animals with normal fear behave.

The other brain mechanism important in emotion is the reticular activating system. This is also shown in Figure 6. This system is located in the stem of the brain and extends forward to the thalamus and hypothalamus. It serves as a general, nonspecific alerting mechanism. It arouses the cortex, facilitates messages coming into the brain from the environment, and tones up the body. It is thought to be involved in consciousness, wakefulness, and excited emotional states. It does not direct behavior in any one direction but has a general energizing effect on all behavior. There is also recent evidence for a deactivating system that produces lowered states of arousal and sleep.

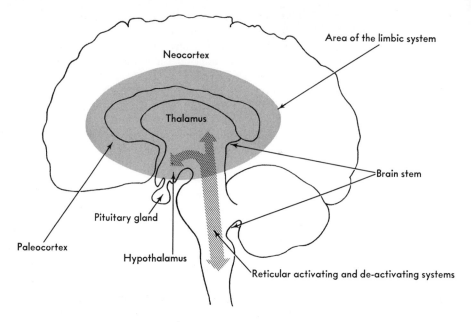

Figure 6. Brain areas important in emotional motivation. The limbic sys-tem—including parts of the paleocortex, thalamus, and hypothalamus—con-tains mechanisms for the bodily expression of fear, rage, and other emotions, as well as the areas for pleasure and pain. It is closely associated with the autonomic nervous system and, through the pituitary gland, the endocrine sys-tem. The reticular activating and deactivating systems control the general level of arousal in the brain and the body.

These brain mechanisms are not fully understood but enough is known now to suggest that emotion is largely a matter of brain functioning. A plau-sible explanation of the events during emotion would be something like this: The sense organs of the body react to a stimulus and this information is trans-mitted to the brain. Various parts of the brain, but particularly the cortex and parts of the limbic system, are involved in appraising the information, particularly in terms of pleasant or unpleasant anticipation. The emotional reaction depends on several mechanisms, with the limbic system controlling the pleasant-unpleasant and approach-avoidance dimensions and the reticular activating system controlling the level of activation, or intensity, dimension. The limbic system is probably the mechanism that most directly influences the visceral reactions through the autonomic nervous system and through the pituitary gland which is closely associated with the hypothalamus. The visceral changes may provide a secondary source of information concerning bodily feelings and this information is then transmitted back to the brain. Thus, the subjective experience of emotion is partly determined by the initial appraisal process and partly by the information coming back from the visceral changes.

An emotion is aroused by an external stimulus. The brain and body respond with an emotional reaction. Now what happens? Action is required! The behavior of the person is affected but, here again, we run into a long-standing controversy over the specific effects of emotion. Some theorists maintain that emotion is different from motivation because emotion has a disorganizing, disrupting effect on behavior. Others maintain that emotion can organize behavior just as a motive does. It is also possible that both emotions and motives can have either organizing or disorganizing effects. We shall first discuss the organizing-disorganizing controversy and then look at fear and anger from a motivational point of view.

Emotions—Organizing or Disorganizing?

In our everyday life we think of emotion as something opposed to reason. A good driver can turn into a dangerous one if he becomes "emotional." A clever lawyer gets an opposition witness upset and then can mix him up so that the testimony is contradictory. It is probably good advice to make major life decisions when one is calm, not excited.

The disorganizing effects of emotion have been studied in experimental situations. For example, Seymour Sarason and his associates have investigated the anxiety school children feel about tests. A scale of test anxiety was developed using questions like "Do you worry a lot while you are taking a test?" On the basis of the answers to this questionnaire, children with very high or very low test anxiety could be selected for intensive study. High-anxiety children did not do well on conventional tests of mental ability, verbal learning, and creative reasoning. These highly anxious children may have ability, but they are too frightened of failure to perform well.

This sort of observation has led Paul T. Young, Donald O. Hebb, and others to conclude that emotions are quite different from motives. But is it true that motives are never disorganizing? Strong motivational states may also disrupt behavior and interfere with good adaptation.

The disorganizing effects of strong motivation have been demonstrated experimentally. Hungry dogs were trained to go to a certain place to get food. Then they were prevented from getting the food by a wire mesh barrier. Moderately hungry dogs learned to go around the barrier to get to the food. On the other hand, extremely hungry dogs strained against the barrier, tried to reach through, and whined. They were unable to pull back and seek another way to get to the food. Their behavior was stereotyped, disruptive, and maladaptive. Of course, one could say that strong motives produce an emotional state, but then one would also have to say that mild emotions produce a motivational state. The important thing is that variables like both hunger and fear can be disruptive at high levels.

Robert Leeper has taken a strong stand against the idea that emotions are necessarily disorganizing. He believes that emotions organize and direct behavior just as motives do. Leeper gives the example of a family who, on returning from a trip, heard about a firebug who had set fire to several homes in the neighborhood. This news raised their anxiety, of course, but what effect did it have on behavior? First of all, it facilitated *perception*—they saw their children's room as a firetrap. The anxiety influenced *verbal behavior* and *symbolic processes*—they talked and thought about little else. The anxiety also increased *learning*—they read catalogs and found out about fire alarm systems. New habits, such as buying a siren, and old habits, such as locking doors, were *performed*. Finally, the anxiety strongly determined the *goals* of the individuals—they talked about the firebug rather than pleasant things and they spent money on the siren rather than something else.

The evidence so far suggests that both emotion and motivation can positively organize and facilitate behavior, at certain times, but they may also disorganize and disrupt behavior. This is a confusing state of affairs. Are there any general principles that will explain this confusion?

Many of the discrepancies can be explained by the Yerkes-Dodson Law described in Chapter 2. Two important factors are involved: the strength of the motive and the difficulty of the task. Behavior is facilitated by a motive up to some strength and then the motive is disorganizing. The exact point of the change depends on the difficulty of the task, with more difficult tasks becoming disorganized at lower levels of motivation. The same principle appears to explain many of the effects of emotion on behavior.

Richard S. Lazarus has reviewed a great many studies on the effects of emotional stress on task performance. Stress was introduced by arranging the test situations so that the subject failed or by complicating the task so that the subject was distracted. The studies, as a whole, indicated that moderate stress facilitates performance but that high stress is disruptive.

In conclusion, emotion may have both organizing and disorganizing effects on behavior. It can disrupt ongoing behavior but it can also produce new, goal-directed forms of behavior. Moderate levels of emotion are generally facilitating but extreme emotion is more disruptive. Some of the effects can be described by the Yerkes-Dodson Law. In all these effects, emotion is very much like motivation, which can also organize or disorganize behavior.

Fear as a Motive

A person can be taught to *escape* from a painful stimulus. A child does so by drawing back after touching a hot stove. With conditioning, the child can also be taught to *avoid* the stove; he draws back at the sight of the stove. In the case of avoidance, the motive is not pain but fear. The fear is aroused by the sight of the stove and the avoidance response reduces the fear. This effect has been demonstrated in a number of laboratory experiments and suggests that fear serves as a motive for learning new responses. Since fear is not an unlearned reaction to the sight of a stove, in this sort of situation it has been described as an *acquired drive*.

The basic experiment demonstrating an acquired drive was done by Neal E. Miller. He studied the acquisition of fear in white rats in the apparatus shown in Figure 7. The animals were first put into the white compartment on the left. Initially, they showed no fear of this neutral compartment. Then, the animals were given a mild shock through the grid floor of the white com-

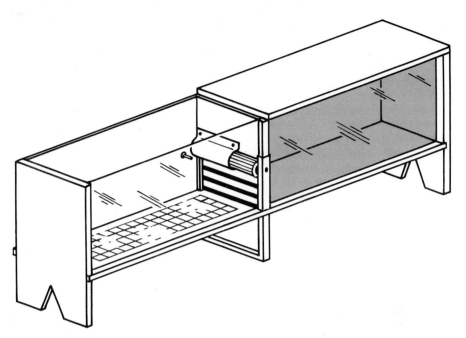

Figure 7. Miller's acquired-drive apparatus. The animal can be shocked through the grid in the white compartment on the left. Access to the safe black compartment on the right requires dropping the sliding door which is painted in horizontal black and white stripes. This can be done by the experimenter pressing a button, or it can be done by the animal pressing the bar on the left side of the white compartment or rotating the wheel above the door. (After N. E. Miller. Studies of fear as an acquirable drive: I. Fear as motivation and fear-reduction as reinforcement in the learning of new responses. J. exp. Psychol., 1948, 38, 89–101.)

partment. Miller allowed the animals to escape from the pain by dropping the sliding door between the two compartments, thus permitting access to the black compartment which had no shock. So far the experiment simply demonstrated that rats will learn to escape from a painful stimulus.

Miller went on to test for an acquired drive. Each animal was put in the white compartment without shock and thus without the primary drive of pain. Recall that there had been no reaction to the white compartment earlier. Now, however, the animals showed fear—trembling, crouching, defecating— as soon as they were put in the white compartment. The stimuli of the white compartment had acquired the power to arouse fear because of the association with the shock. Fear of the white compartment was learned.

Does this learned fear fulfill the key definition of a drive in that it will motivate new learning? Miller tested for this by keeping the sliding door between the compartments closed but wiring it so that it would drop open if the rat rotated a little wheel above it. The fearful rats would try many responses but eventually would touch and move the little wheel. When the door dropped the rats scampered into the black compartment. On subsequent trials they continued to perform the wheel-turning response. Thus, the fear motivated the learning of a new response and the fear-reduction, which was apparent when the rat reached the black compartment, served as a reward.

Miller further tested fear as a motive by disconnecting the wheel from the door so that wheel turning no longer caused the door to drop. Instead a little bar was rigged up so that pressing it would trigger the door. The animals, under these conditions, eventually stopped turning the wheel and learned to press the bar. Therefore, the specific response is not important—the critical factor is whether the response leads to fear-reduction.

The anxiety aroused by a personal threat also operates as a motive. People learn various responses to avoid anxiety, but on the human level these are called *defense mechanisms*. Repression is such a mechanism. As we saw in Chapter 2, a person may not be able to remember material associated with an anxiety-arousing experience. The function of a repression can be seen in the famous case of Anna O., treated by Freud's early collaborator Breuer. This young woman had to tend her father day and night during a long terminal illness. One evening, as she heard music from a neighbor's party, she had the momentary wish that her father would die soon. Anna was so shocked by this fleeting thought that she immediately repressed it. The repression enabled her to maintain her belief that she had only love for her father and avoid the anxiety associated with the death wish.

Anxiety, if it is not too great, can also motivate mature and adaptive responses. A student can react to a low mid-term grade by studying harder. A man who is heartily disliked by all his associates can examine his own behavior to see what he is doing to provoke hostility. This sort of self-examination is not easy to do, of course, and may require psychotherapy. Nevertheless, there are those who maintain that a moderate degree of anxiety can be a positive force for a person, motivating creative responses and personal growth.

Anger as a Motive

The original frustration-aggression hypothesis was stated in very strong terms—every frustration produces an aggressive tendency and every aggression can be traced to a frustration. We know now that there can be other responses to frustration—a *regression* to childish behavior, apathetic *withdrawal,* or, even, quietly effective *problem-solving* behavior. The confusion here seems to be between the arousal of an emotion, the emotional reaction itself, and the response that is motivated by the emotion. It would be clearer, perhaps, if we define *frustration* as the emotionally arousing condition, *anger* as the intervening emotional state, and *aggression* as one of many responses to anger.

Judson Brown has reviewed a number of studies which show that introducing a frustration in a learning situation increases the vigor of responding and facilitates performance. In one study, A. Amsel and J. Roussel trained rats to go down a long alley. Halfway down the alley was a goal box in which the hungry animals were given a food pellet. After eating this, they were allowed to continue down the second half of the alley to a second goal box where they were given a second pellet of food. After the animals learned the sequence, the experimenters introduced frustration trials, which consisted of omitting the food pellet in the first goal box. The results showed that when the pellet was omitted from the first goal box, the rats ran down the second half of the alley *faster* than they ordinarily did. In other words, the frustration increased their motivation to get to the second goal box.

Now it is true that an aggressive response is frequently learned as the appropriate reaction for reducing anger or the frustration-induced drive. Florence Goodenough, years ago, showed that the frequency of temper tantrums, or aggressive outbursts, in a child is proportional to the number of times adults yield to him. In other words, the child is rewarded for this behavior. Mice can be trained to be ferocious fighters, who will attack other mice without provocation, by giving them a series of easy successes early in life—the same way a fight manager brings along a professional boxer by setting up easy matches. Mice can be trained to be peace-loving by picking them up and gentling them whenever they show aggression. Thus, aggression can be learned as a response.

Actually, aggression is not a very effective way to attain goals in social living. It may work for a child with overly permissive parents but, in most social situations, it leads to retaliation eventually. John Dollard has described the spiralling effect of aggression in a social group when one person starts, another retaliates, the first one fights back, and so on. There are obvious parallels in large organizations, international relations, and, even, academic communities. There are more effective ways for frustrated individuals to react—problem-solving, increased communication, and social cooperation.

A person may be frustrated, feel angry, and have an aggressive tendency but still not show aggression because of *inhibition.* The inhibition may be due to a fear of punishment or social disapproval. Many middle-class children in our society are extremely inhibited about aggression. Inhibition may only serve to increase frustration so that there is a likelihood of sudden outbursts. For example, the South African government responded to racial unrest by ever tighter restrictions so that the situation has become increasingly explosive.

Inhibited aggression does not simply go away but seeks an outlet. Aggression may be expressed indirectly by backbiting or by sullenness. By the mechanism of *displacement,* it may also be expressed towards someone other than the person responsible for the frustration. Thus, a harassed executive may take it out on his wife or an economically frustrated worker may blame his misfortunes on the Jews, Negroes, or foreigners.

The Yale frustration-aggression theorists also suggested that when a person is frustrated and all possible outlets are effectively blocked, the aggression can be *turned against the self* in the form of self-hatred, self-criticism, and suicide. Recall that, when frustrated, some of the students in Funkenstein's experiment turned the anger inward and became depressed. Still, not everyone does this. It seems to depend on the extent to which a person blames himself as the cause of the frustration. It also seems to depend on the degree to which the depressed person believes his depressive behavior will achieve his goals in relation to other people. At least clinically, the depressed person may feel that he is punishing others and the suicide frequently thinks his act will convince others of his suffering. Thus, even depression and suicide can be viewed as goal-directed responses.

In summary, frustration induces an emotional motive which we have called anger. This motive is directed towards overcoming obstacles in the way of goal attainment rather than towards destruction for its own sake. Responses that lead to the original goal and reduce both the original motivation and the frustration-induced motivation may be learned. These responses include aggression, regression, depression, and problem-solving.

Intrinsically
Motivated Behavior

The other day I watched my one-and-a-half-year-old daughter play in the back-yard. She was incredibly busy and quite serious. She wandered about, picking up a great variety of objects— twigs, stones, toys, an old bathing sandal, a garden tool, a piece of burlap, my discarded magazine, and the cat as he wandered through. Each one was handled, examined, and tried out for various purposes. A peal of laughter from the neighbor's brought her toddling to the fence to peer at the older children. She decided to try the sliding board and, when she had trouble getting up the rungs, I went over to help, but, in her independence, she pushed

6

me away. She finally succeeded and slid down with a look of pleasure and triumph. This is strongly motivated behavior.

What is the nature of the motivation for all these activities? There is no known homeostatic imbalance, no tension-arousing stimulus in the ordinary sense, and no simple hormonal condition. The behavior does not seem to depend directly on the homeostatic, sexual, or emotional motives we have discussed so far.

The classical instinct theorists assumed that certain kinds of sensory experiences and behavioral activities are innately rewarding, that exploratory, playful, and other activities are engaged in for their own sake, for some inherent pleasure or satisfaction. Charles Darwin, William James, and William McDougall all spoke of curiosity as a basic instinct. James added play.

During the reaction against the instinct theorists in the twenties, the innate basis of motives for curiosity, play, and so on was challenged by many psychologists. For example, E. J. Kempf assumed that there are only three basic organic cravings—those related to nutrition, sex, and fear. In his view, these are the primary drives and all others derive from them. Thus, a hungry animal may learn to search for food in all sorts of nooks and crannies. After a while this activity gives the appearance of an independent curiosity motive, but it is always traceable to hunger and ultimately dependent on it. So, too, playfulness, creativity, and general activity are said to be derived from more basic drives.

Nevertheless, in recent years there has been a swing away from the derived-motivation explanation of curiosity and related behavior. Theories of derived motives have been found increasingly to be inadequate. New evidence suggests that some of these motives are indeed innate. In this chapter, we shall first describe the theories of derived motivation, then present the new evidence for various kinds of independent motives, and, finally, discuss some of the theoretical implications of these findings.

CONCEPTS OF DERIVED MOTIVES

To say that a motive is "derived" from a more basic physiological one is to say very little. What is needed is an explanation of the process—a description of the method of derivation. In this section we shall consider the three most important theories outlining such a method of derivation. The first is Sigmund Freud's idea that sexual and aggressive motives are transformed into cultural ones by the mechanism of *sublimation*. The second is Gordon Allport's concept of *functional autonomy* in which some motives become detached from their physiological origins. Finally, Neal E. Miller's theory of *acquired drives and rewards* attempts to show how new motives may be learned on the basis of association with physiological drives and rewards. As we go along we shall also point out some of the weaknesses in these theories.

The first important theo-
rist to suggest that some motives are derived from more basic biological
ones was Sigmund Freud. The higher cultural attainments of man—science,
art, ethics, religion—did not impress Freud very much. He saw man as a
biological organism seething with primitive instinctual forces kept in check
by the thin veneer of civilization. Cultural attainments, for him, were mere
compromises or safety valves in the inevitable conflict between basic sexual
and aggressive motives and the restrictions of society.

Sublimation is the deflecting of an impulse away from its original purpose
into an activity that is more socially acceptable. It starts out as a defense
against an impulse which is forbidden by society in general or parents in
particular. For example, many children have a desire to play with and smear
their feces. Parents, in general, react somewhat negatively to this activity.
One method of resolving this conflict is to deflect the impulse to smear into
an activity like painting. Painting is very popular in nursery schools and
young children use the paint in a smearing way. This is still not true sublimation but a simple substitution. However, if a child continues to develop
an interest in creative painting, it may serve as an outlet for his impulses
and eventually become divorced from the original smearing tendency. The
smearing tendency is now said to be sublimated into the higher social activity
of painting.

All kinds of primitive sexual and aggressive impulses may be sublimated.
An infantile wish to exhibit one's body may be sublimated into professional
acting. Sexual curiosity may be transformed into scientific research. A sadistic
tendency may find a socially useful outlet in surgery. A. A. Brill mentions a
patient who before treatment got into trouble with the law because of his
voyeuristic, or Peeping Tom, activities, but then was able to sublimate his
urges in a new job selling optical instruments.

The most cogent criticism of the concept of sublimation has come from
within the psychoanalytic camp. Heinz Hartmann and his associates have
developed a new *ego psychology* to replace Freud's explanation of the development of interests, hobbies, and creative work. Observations of children
suggest that certain *ego functions*—such as grasping, walking, perceiving,
and thinking—develop *autonomously* in the child; that is, they are not dependent on sexual and aggressive motives. Later, they *may* become involved
with these motives, as when the athletic performance of a son becomes of
great importance to a father. Even, then, the ego-functions may later on
become *secondarily autonomous*, as when the son outgrows his dependence
on his father's approval. Thus, the scientist, the artist, or the professional is
very likely engaging in activities that either always were or have become free
from sexual or aggressive impulses.

Functional Autonomy

The second important
theory of the derivation of motives is Gordon Allport's concept of functional
autonomy. Allport was reacting to the theories of both McDougall and
Freud. He did not believe that adult human behavior is motivated entirely

by instincts that are fixed from birth, as suggested by McDougall, nor did he accept the Freudian idea that adult interests grow out of the sublimations of infantile sexual and aggressive impulses. He did accept the idea that an infant is motivated by a few primitive physiological drives but that somehow adult motives become divorced from these early origins and function independently in the pursuit of contemporary goals—that is, they become functionally autonomous.

Allport's most famous example is the ex-sailor who longs for the sea. Originally he may have gone to sea in order to make money and earn a living. In this sense, his sea-going behavior was motivated by something as simple as hunger. Now, perhaps, he is a wealthy banker able to fulfill his hunger needs many times over. Yet he retains a nostalgia for the sea, perhaps he hangs seascapes in his office, and his love of the sea may be more intense than it ever was when he was an active sailor. Thus, the love of the sea has become completely divorced from the early hunger motive but continues to exist as an even more powerful force in the personality.

Again, we come to the critical question of the exact mechanism whereby a basic physiological motive gives rise to habits that become functionally autonomous motives. It is quite clear that the physiological motives in childhood lead to a great variety of responses but that only a few of them become functionally autonomous. Allport's explanation is that only habits-in-the-making have motivating qualities. "Motives are always a kind of striving for some form of completion," according to Allport. A child learning to speak, walk, or dress is so motivated, as is the adult with an unfinished task. Still, this mechanism does not appear to account for the persisting life-long autonomous motives with which we are mostly concerned. After all, the child does learn to walk and tasks are usually completed. Allport's answer is that, although muscular skills are often perfected, the great tasks of life—art, science, and religion—are by their very nature never to be fully completed. Therefore, there is always motivation in these areas.

The functional autonomy theory has been criticized by many people, perhaps most effectively by Peter Bertocci. Bertocci suggests that the process Allport describes as a habit becoming functionally autonomous is really a switching of a habit from an old drive to a new one. The habit does not become free from all drives, it serves new masters. He gives the analogy of a horseman switching from one horse to another.

Bertocci agrees with Allport that the ex-sailor who loves the sea is not motivated by something as simple as the remnant of a hunger motive. But, he says, one has to assume that the love of the sea has become divorced from all original motives only if one assumes that the person was only motivated by hunger to begin with. Bertocci suggests that the young sailor may have also been motivated by basic drives for gregariousness, self-assertion, and curiosity. Now, when the paunchy, middle-aged banker looks at his seascapes, he is flooded with memories of the rough humor of his shipmates, the excitement of heavy storms, and the scent of oriental ports. The old motives may still be with him, but they are unfulfilled as he leads his routinized life, separated from people by ranks of secretaries and walled in by oak panels from the adventures of life. No wonder he longs for the sea!

The most systematic at-
tempt to explain how secondary motives are derived from physiological ones
is Neal E. Miller's theory of acquired drives and rewards. This theory differs
from the other two in that great emphasis is placed on the mechanism of
derivation and experimental verification is attempted. The basic idea is that
a neutral stimulus which is paired with the onset of a primary drive will come
to arouse a drive by itself. So, too, a neutral stimulus associated with a primary
reward will acquire some reward value of its own.

You will recall that Miller's basic experiment on fear as an acquired
motive was presented in the chapter on emotional motives. In the apparatus
shown earlier in Figure 7, Miller associated the white compartment with an
electric shock and the escape to the black compartment with reduction in pain.
Later, when animals were placed in the white compartment without shock,
they showed an acquired fear. They would learn to make a response to get to
the black compartment where they were rewarded by a reduction in fear. Thus,
the white compartment became an acquired source of fear motivation and the
black compartment functioned as an acquired reward.

The acquisition of an acquired reward based on a positive motive like
hunger was demonstrated in studies by Wolfe and Cowles with chimpanzees.
Poker chips ordinarily have little value for chimpanzees. However, if they
are taught to insert them into a vending machine to obtain grapes, the chips
become highly prized rewards. The chimpanzees will learn to pull a handle
or select the right box in order to get the chips, even if they cannot turn the
chips in for food until the end of the day's session. It should be noted, however, that the reward-value of the poker chips depends on the hunger of the
chimpanzees and obtaining grapes from the vending machine. In this regard
the chips are like money—during an economic inflation money, too, loses a
good deal of its trade-in value.

The theory of acquired motivation has not been without its critics.
Judson Brown has pointed out that only fear really fulfills the requirements
of an acquired motive. The fear drive is aroused by a stimulus, it is a learned
response to that stimulus, it facilitates responding, and its reduction functions
as a reward. The same analysis, however, cannot be extended to something
like an acquired motive for money or tokens. There is no doubt that money
functions as an acquired *reward*. But what is the acquired *drive* which the reward reduces? That is, there is no stimulus, analogous to a fear stimulus,
which arouses a desire for money. So, too, depriving someone of money
before he has learned the value of it does not set up a "drive for money."
Brown suggests that the acquired reward-value of a coin or a token is
dependent on other drives like hunger or anxiety.

Neal Miller brings up the same problem in a slightly different context.
He notes that all the studies demonstrating acquired *drive* are based on
negative motives like pain. Although acquired *rewards* may be based on
positive motives like hunger, no study clearly demonstrates an acquired *drive*
based on hunger. Miller, himself, has been unable to do so in spite of numerous attempts. For example, Arlo Myers along with Miller attempted to
demonstrate an acquired drive based on hunger in the same apparatus used to

Intrinsically
Motivated
Behavior

demonstrate acquired fear. Rats were placed in the white compartment, when hungry, and could enter the black compartment by simply touching the door which then slid down automatically. In the black compartment they were allowed to eat a food pellet. Different groups were given 70, 30, 10, and 0 trials of this sort of training. Thus, the cues of the white box were associated with being hungry and the cues of the black box with hunger-reduction.

The subsequent test for a learned drive based on hunger was parallel to the earlier study on acquired fear. First, the animals were thoroughly satiated with food and water for several weeks. Then, they were placed in the white compartment. This is like putting the rats in without the electric shock. The door to the black compartment could no longer be opened by touching. Now it could only be opened by a new response—pressing a bar. If an acquired drive based on hunger was operating, then it would be expected that the groups with the greatest number of training trials would learn to press the bar more quickly. Certainly, the group with no training trials would not be expected to show any learning since there was no opportunity for a drive to be acquired. The results, however, showed no differences between the groups in learning to press the bar. All groups learned equally well. Thus, no additional drive was acquired on the basis of the hunger.

An interesting side light of the Myers and Miller experiment is that the control group—those with no feeding experience in the black box—learned to press the bar in order to enter the black compartment. Recall that these animals were satiated on food and water so that they were not motivated by hunger or thirst. Myers and Miller conclude that the animals were motivated by an "exploratory" drive.

EVIDENCE FOR INTRINSICALLY MOTIVATED BEHAVIOR

We have seen that the various theories of derived motivation—sublimation, functional autonomy, and acquired drives and rewards—have certain weaknesses. It is difficult to explain a good deal of human behavior with these theories. Not that curiosity, exploration, and the like can never be learned on the basis of motives like hunger, sex, and parental approval. A rat *can* be trained to be a great explorer by placing his food in various hidden places. A child's sexual curiosity *can* be made intense by making the matter forbidden. A boy's interest in athletics *can* be heightened by his father's approval.

Here we must make a distinction between *extrinsic* and *intrinsic* motivation. Almost any response can be learned and performed on the basis of a reward such as food or approval, including exploration and play. In such situations the reward is extrinsic to the activity—there is no inherent connection between the activity and the reward. The activity is performed *in order to* get the reward. Exploration, play, and other activities, however, may also be intrinsically rewarding—they may be engaged in for their own sake, for some inherent pleasure or satisfaction. Extrinsic rewards cannot account for the playful sort of behavior shown by my daughter in the backyard. Much of this activity seems intrinsically motivated.

Intrinsically
Motivated
Behavior

74

In this section we shall present the evidence for several new kinds of motives—sensory, curiosity, activity, manipulatory, and cognitive. These appear to be independent of other motives, they are not learned on the basis of simpler drives, and they involve behavior which is intrinsically motivating. We shall call them intrinsic motives.

Sensory Motives

The classical thories of motivation have assumed that an organism basically seeks to reduce stimulation. This view is seen in Clark Hull's behavior theory in which drive stimuli from within or without the organism goad it into action until some means is found to eliminate the drive. A reward, then, consists of reducing drive and its accompanying stimuli. The same idea is found in Freud's psychoanalytic theory, in which the function of the brain is to reduce or abolish all forms of stimulation. The ultimate goal here is a state of nirvana—a condition in which there is no stimulation.

There is no doubt that people seek to avoid excessive environmental stimulation and inner tension. By summertime, most city dwellers are ready to leave the noise of traffic, the pressures of work, and the chatter of cocktail parties for the peace and quiet of the country. But sooner or later, the average vacationer begins to be bored and starts thinking of the excitement again —new projects, new ideas, new things to talk about. People seem to seek neither an absence nor an excess but an optimal level of stimulation with some variation in it.

The intense desire for environmental stimulation in human beings is dramatically illustrated in the <i>sensory deprivation</i> studies begun at McGill University. College students were offered what appeared to be an ideal job. They were paid $20 a day to do nothing—absolutely nothing! They lay on a comfortable bed in a small compartment as shown in Figure 8. Their

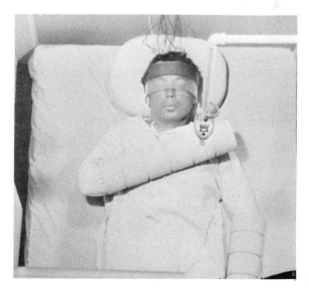

Figure 8. Subject in a sensory-deprivation experiment. Cuffs over hands prevent touch. Plastic goggles admit diffuse light but permit no perception of shape. Ordinarily a foam-rubber cushion covers the ears but here it is replaced with EEG apparatus. An air conditioner on the ceiling masks sounds and reduces temperature sensations. The subject reports his experiences into the microphone. (Photo from Gateways to the Mind, Bell System Science Series film.)

translucent goggles admitted only a diffuse light. Cardboard cuffs covered their hands, preventing touch. Sounds were masked by the hum of an air-conditioner and a foam rubber head piece. Except for brief intervals for eating, going to the toilet, and taking tests, they simply did nothing. However, theories notwithstanding, the students found this nirvana intolerable. They wanted stimulation so badly that they would ask to hear a recording of an old stock market report over and over. Although they were asked to stay as long as possible, most subjects could take it for only two or three days. They preferred to work harder, at less pay, in a stimulating environment.

Many subjects had peculiar experiences during the sensory deprivation period. At first, they tried thinking about personal and intellectual problems, but after a while they could not concentrate or sustain a train of thought. They had periods of confusion, irritability, and stress. Finally, they began having visual hallucinations—dots of light would appear, then geometrical patterns and, eventually vivid scenes. These effects disappeared after the experiment was terminated.

Curiosity Motives

The search for stimuli is not random. One important aspect of stimulation that arouses the interest of people is *novelty*. Novelty can be defined in terms of the amount and degree of previous experience with a stimulus. Sometimes it is hard to say how novel a stimulus is because we do not always know the complete background of a person. Nevertheless, to the extent that a stimulus is novel, it arouses *curiosity* in an animal, a child, or an adult. If the stimulus is too novel or too suddenly presented, it may arouse fear and avoidance instead.

An experiment reported by Salvatore Maddi illustrates the motivation for a moderate degree of novelty. Nursery school children were allowed to play with a group of eight small toys on a table. Then they were allowed to pick one of five other tables of toys for additional play. One of these tables contained the same eight toys (0 per cent novelty); another contained six old toys and two new ones (25 per cent novelty); the third, four old and four new (50 per cent novelty); the next, two old and six new (75 per cent novelty); and the last one, all new toys (100 per cent novelty). The children, as a group, selected the tables with 25 to 75 per cent novelty. They avoided the extremes of complete familiarity or complete novelty.

Although novelty is the most striking feature of the stimuli that evoke curiosity, several other features are important. With degree of familiarity held constant, children show more curiosity to stimuli that are intense, colored, or complex. Daniel Berlyne has also shown that the element of surprise is important. For example, if a series of triangular designs is followed by a circular one, more curiosity is aroused. So, too, more curiosity is shown to an unexpected, incongruous picture of a lion with an elephant's head. Some investigators view all these features as aspects of novelty.

Some of these variables are involved in our adult appreciation of music, art, and poetry. In a great symphony, there are many variations on themes and unexpected passages, which are all resolved during the movement. A great modern painter, like Picasso, deliberately introduces novelty, discordance, and incongruity—perhaps too much so for the average person. Close study of a Picasso, however, will reveal a subtle harmony and resolution. Read a Shakespeare sonnet and notice the resolution in the last two lines. With the proper training, people find these high-level games of enormous satisfaction.

All things pall after a while. People get tired of Tchaikovsky and move on to Bach. This is the process of *habituation*. Novelty decreases with repeated exposure. Presenting a familiar stimulus to a child results in boredom or even aversion. The more novel or complex a stimulus is, the longer habituation takes. After habituation takes place and the stimulus is not presented for a period of time, *recovery* may occur. Recovery depends on how novel the stimulus was to begin with, the amount of exposure, and the time since the last exposure. A stimulus may return to its original level of interest. After ten years, even Tchaikovsky may arouse curiosity.

Curiosity is found in very young children. Jean Piaget, the great Swiss developmental psychologist, observed curiosity in his three-month-old son, Laurent. Piaget suspended a rattle above his crib and attached a string. Laurent spent 15 minutes shaking the rattle and laughing uproariously. No extrinsic rewards were involved here.

Curiosity in monkeys has been studied by Robert Butler and his associates. Each monkey in these studies was placed in a dimly lit, opaque box with two small, covered windows. The set-up is shown in Figure 9. One window was

Figure 9.   Rhesus monkey in visual exploration apparatus. The monkey learns to push open the unlocked window in order to see out for 30 seconds. (Based on descriptions in R. A. Butler. Discrimination learning by Rhesus monkeys to visual-exploration motivation. J. comp. physiol. Psychol., *1953, 46, 95–98.)*

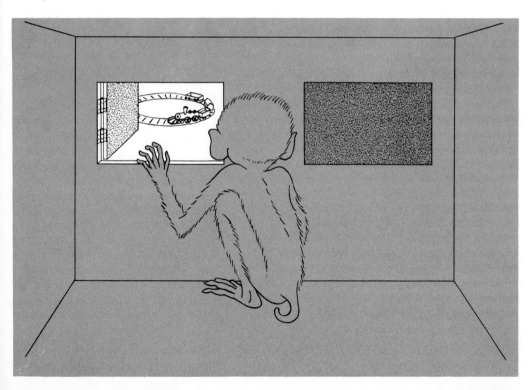

colored yellow and the other blue, with the yellow always locked and the blue unlocked. If the monkey pushed against the blue window it would swing open and permit a view of the laboratory room for 30 seconds. The monkeys not only learned this response for the reward of visual exploration but also showed remarkably little satiation or habituation. One group of monkeys was tested for ten hours a day for six days and showed a fairly constant visual exploration for about 40 per cent of the time.

The strength of this motive depends on the nature of the visual stimulus. The window-opening was less frequent when the reward was an empty room than when a toy train was operating. The strongest reward was the sight of another monkey. Sounds were also rewarding. Monkeys responded to hear the train or a monkey, but less frequently than they did to see the train or monkey. Not all stimuli were rewarding. The monkeys did not learn the response in order to see a large dog or hear a monkey in pain.

Curiosity in monkeys also depends on the amount of stimulus deprivation. Butler deprived monkeys of visual experience for zero, two, four, and eight hours. The reward was a twelve-second look at the monkey colony. Responding increased with deprivation up to four hours and then leveled off. This experiment shows that there is some internal drive for novel stimulation—probably related to brain functioning—which is built up over time.

Activity and Manipulatory Motives

In addition to having motives for sensory stimulation and novel stimuli, a developing child is motivated to *do* things—to run, climb, throw, jump, hold, drop, open, and close. This is nowhere more dramatically seen than in the young child's struggle to walk. The child pulls himself up, stumbles a few steps, falls, pulls himself up again, and tries again. This universal struggle is not rewarded in any simple extrinsic way—in fact, the child suffers pain and is initially less successful in getting things than he was by crawling. Parental approval does not seem to be the critical factor in learning to walk.

Young children also spend a great deal of time in manipulatory activities like putting on and taking off a ring. Harry F. Harlow and his associates have demonstrated a manipulatory motive in the monkey. In these studies, a mechanical puzzle, like that shown in Figure 10, is placed in a monkey's cage. Monkeys learned to disassemble this sort of puzzle with persistent work. The number of correct responses increased over a period of 12 daily tests until near perfection was reached. The novelty of the stimuli *per se* must have worn off before then, so the primary motive was to master the manipulatory problem.

Interest in mechanical puzzles can be reduced by satiation, in which the puzzles are kept in the cage for a long block of time. In a ten-hour satiation procedure, Harlow found that the number of devices in the puzzle that were opened declined. The satiation effects seem to be similar to habituation to novel stimuli.

In these studies no extrinsic reward was used. Subsequently, however, it was shown that adding a food reward for solving the problem did not make the learning more efficient. Instead the general behavior changed. The food-rewarded animals used the puzzle only to get food and had little interest in

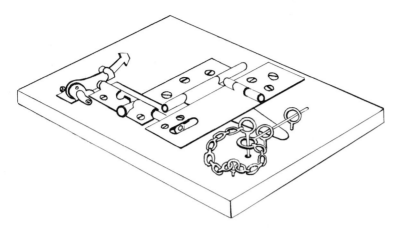

Figure 10. Six-device mechanical puzzle used for studying manipulatory motivation in monkeys. Monkeys learn to disassemble puzzles without extrinsic reward. (After H. F. Harlow. Learning and satiation of response in intrinsically motivated complex puzzle performance by monkeys. J. comp. physiol. Psychol., 1950, 43, 289–294.)

manipulation for manipulation's sake. This may be what happens when an intrinsically rewarding activity is turned into a response to get an extrinsic reward. Young children are notoriously eager to learn to do things. This eagerness is soon lost after exposure to formal education. One reason may be that the intrinsically rewarding activity of learning is transformed into a response to get good grades, win the approval of teachers and parents, and get into college where one can meet an eligible man or get a good start in the business world.

Cognitive Motives

The motives described so far in this chapter can be thought of as involving the pleasurable use of one's perceptual apparatus and one's muscular apparatus. Why not, then, such a use of one's thinking apparatus? The cognitive functions are those involved in thinking, symbolizing, and problem-solving. Children find these activities fun —they love riddles, rhymes, and mental games. They love to solve problems and, if they are not inhibited by cultural attitudes, to play with numbers. Even jaded adults enjoy crossword puzzles, bridge, and problem-solving. For many scientists, engineers, businessmen, physicians, artisans, and others, the real pleasure in work is the meeting of challenges and the solution of tough problems.

Of course, thinking, remembering, and other cognitive processes operate in the service of motives like hunger, anxiety, and the need for approval. A number of examples were given in Chapter 2. The use of the intellect can be intrinsically satisfying; however, as with Harlow's manipulating monkeys, the pleasure can be taken out of intrinsically motivated cognitive processes by making them means to serve an extrinsic end.

Intrinsically
Motivated
Behavior

One specific facet of cognitive motivation has received some attention from psychologists in recent years. Although this is only one aspect of the process, it may mark the beginning of an era of exploration into various aspects of cognitive motivation. The specific facet to which we refer is the motivation to be logical, internally consistent, so that various thought processes are congruent with one another. This notion has been most fully developed by Leon Festinger and his associates in the theory of *cognitive dissonance.*

According to Festinger, specific ideas or bits of information known to a person may or may not be consistent with one another. If they are consistent, then a state of consonance, or agreement, exists and there is no problem. However, if two bits of information are inconsistent or mutually contradictory, then a state of dissonance occurs which is uncomfortable and motivates the person to reduce dissonance and gain consonance.

Festinger gives the example of the person who (1) knows that smoking is bad for him but (2) continues to smoke. As Festinger puts it:*

. . . the person who continues to smoke, knowing that it is bad for his health, may also feel (a) he enjoys smoking so much it is worth it; (b) the chances of his health suffering are not as serious as some would make out; (c) he can't always avoid every possible dangerous contingency and still live; and (d) perhaps even if he stopped smoking he would put on weight which is equally bad for his health. So, continuing to smoke is, after all, consistent with his ideas about smoking.

In this example, cognitive dissonance motivated the rationalizations. The Festinger group has presented evidence for the cognitive dissonance theory in a variety of situations. For example, when a person finally makes a decision between two close alternatives, a state of dissonance occurs. Thus, a man who buys one automobile, after considering several other attractive makes, may be plagued with the feeling that one of the others might have been better. One study showed that he attempts to reduce this dissonance by actively seeking out information consonant with his decision and ignoring dissonant information. People who had recently purchased a new car were shown issues of magazines and newspapers they regularly read that had appeared since the purchase. They were asked to indicate which automobile advertisements they had noticed and which they had read. The results showed that, of the ads that they noticed, they read 65 per cent of those concerning the cars they had purchased and only 40 per cent of those concerning makes they had considered but not purchased. This selectivity in receiving new information helped bolster their decision and reduce dissonance.

Obviously, we are dealing here with a very complex phenomenon. Other factors would also be expected to influence opinions and beliefs. Nevertheless, the motivation to gain internal cognitive consistency seems to be real enough. An important question remaining is to what extent is this motive learned? Certainly learning is involved in the acquisition of cognitive symbols and belief systems. Still, the Festinger group believes that, however the thoughts are acquired, the dissonance between thoughts is as basic a motive as any other. Future research will be needed to answer this question.

* L. Festinger. *A theory of cognitive dissonance.* Stanford: Stanford University Press, 1957, p. 2.

The discovery—or really rediscovery—of intrinsically motivated behavior has produced a re-examination of basic concepts in the field of motivation. The idea that all motives are derived from internal homeostatic imbalance—which, as we have seen, does not really account for hunger, sex, or similar motives perfectly—runs into great difficulty in explaining the intrinsic motives.

This difficulty led Robert S. Woodworth—one of the most distinguished psychologists of this century—to reject *need-primacy* theories, like Clark Hull's and Sigmund Freud's, that place exclusive importance on internal needs. Instead, Woodworth proposed a *behavior-primacy* theory of motivation in which the emphasis is on the organism *dealing with the environment.* The intrinsic curiosity, manipulatory, and other motives described in this chapter would be examples of motivation to learn to deal with the environment.

In an important paper, Robert White has taken a similar position. To him, all the specific intrinsic motives are aspects of an over-all *effectance* motive. This motive originates only in the brain, not in visceral imbalance, has no specific consummatory response, and is not rewarded by tension- or stimulus-reduction. The biological function of effectance motivation is to attain *competence* in dealing with the environment. Of course, a child at play is not aware of this biological goal but is simply having fun. The analogy to sexual activities is clear: The biological function is species reproduction, but the behavior is motivated in the individual by pleasure-seeking.

We have already seen that in the psychoanalytic school the ego-psychologists like Heinz Hartmann and his collaborators have rejected the Freudian doctrine of sublimation. Ego-functions are now considered primarily autonomous. Even if they do get linked with sexual and aggressive motives, they may again become autonomous at a later time.

None of the theories mentioned so far—behavior primacy, effectance motivation, or ego-autonomy—implies that these new motives supplant the well-established homeostatic or sexual ones. Instead, the idea is that the great bulk of day-to-day activity (of the child, especially) is motivated intrinsically in a steady, undramatic fashion, with the more insistent motives like hunger taking over for relatively brief periods.

The intrinsic motives for stimulation and activity appear to be innate, with learning playing only a secondary role. Therefore, these intrinsic motives offer some support for the instinct family of motivational theories. Similarly, since pleasure seems to be involved in exploring and manipulating, while pain and fear may be aroused by the stimuli that are avoided, the newer hedonistic theories of motivation are quite congruent with these intrinsic motives.

Harry F. Harlow has suggested that intrinsic motives, like the others, depend on brain centers stimulated through the sense organs. Harlow suggests that traditional motives, like hunger, arise from stimulation from interoceptors (he mentions receptors in the stomach, but receptors in the hypothalamus could be added), while intrinsic motives arise from exteroceptors, like the eye. Both would activate brain centers. As we saw in earlier chapters, homeostatic, sexual and maternal, and emotional motives are quite dependent on brain centers. Specific brain centers for the intrinsic motives have not yet been established. Donald B. Lindsley suggested that the reticular activating system is involved. The limbic system might also be involved since intrinsic motives involve pleasure and pain. We shall have to wait for more research to understand the physiological bases of intrinsic motives, but they could very well be similar to those for the traditional motives.

It is also possible that traditional drive theory could accommodate these results. The reaction to stimuli is not indiscriminate, but depends, in part, on the state of the brain—especially its level of functioning prior to testing for curiosity or activity. As Judson Brown points out, it is not correct to say that the curiosity of Butler's monkeys is *aroused* by the stimulus, since the monkeys pushed open the window *before* seeing the stimulus. Some condition like "boredom" might be the "drive" behind some of these intrinsic motives. Recall that Butler's monkeys were more motivated after sensory deprivation. A modification of drive theory to include these special deprivation conditions might be able to explain intrinsic motivation.

To bring the discussion around full circle, is it possible that intrinsic motives have some homeostatic consequences after all? Certainly not the old homeostatic concept as it applies to visceral functioning. But is it not possible to extend the idea of homeostasis to brain functioning? This is implied by Lindsley when he says that a certain level of stimulation is required for normal brain functioning. The cognitive disturbances during sensory deprivation would support this. Other evidence, presented by Donald Hebb, indicates that stimulation and activity are necessary in infancy for normal perceptual development. It is possible, then, that brain mechanisms mediating intrinsic motives serve to assure the proper development and functioning of the brain, thereby facilitating adjustment to the environment.

To conclude, the demonstration of intrinsically motivated behavior has raised questions about traditional theories of motivation. New concepts— behavior-primacy, effectance motivation, and ego-autonomy—have been suggested. The intrinsic motives are quite consistent with instinct and hedonistic theories of motivation and might possibly be explained by modifications of drive theory. Intrinsic motives may be shown—sometime in the future—to involve brain mechanisms and functions analogous to those of the traditional motives.

Origins
of Social Motivation

Let us consider a young man just entering college—full of bright hopes and great expectations. Why has he decided to spend four years of his life reading books, writing papers, and listening to lectures when he could get a job, get married, and provide for all of his physiological motives? Going to college cannot be explained on the basis of hunger, thirst, or even sex.

It is possible of course, that the student is motivated by an intrinsic curiosity motive—an unquenchable thirst for knowledge. This may be true for some, but most students have had this intrinsic motivation inhibited by

83

7

years of dreary schooling or the general cultural antagonism to intellectual pursuits. Therefore, intrinsic curiosity cannot explain the intense, sometimes desperate, desire to go to college.

If we asked the young man, he might say that going to college was expected of him—he would disappoint his parents if he did not go. Actually, this claim is rather startling—a motive stemming from the wishes of others. He might also say that he wants to get ahead in this world, to be a successful executive. Certainly this goal is not necessary to satisfy hunger nor is it a way of avoiding fatigue since executives work much harder than their employees. The desire for money perhaps? This is important but it does not explain why a millionaire continues to work compulsively long after he has enough money to satisfy his physiological needs many times over. There is something new here—prestige, status, self-esteem.

Perhaps the young man will say, frankly, that he is out to have a good time in college. What this means, essentially, is having fun with people—the dates, the fraternity parties, the football games. How can we explain the thrill people evidently get from a winning football team? Later on the young man may complain that the classes are so large that he does not "get to know" the professors. There is an unfulfilled motive, here, for a special kind of social interaction.

All these motives involve people—being with them, gaining their approval, having fun with them, competing against them, enhancing one's self-esteem with them or through them. This interaction with other people is why we call these social motives. Social behavior cannot be fully explained by hunger, sex, and pain, nor even by effectance. In fact, social motives often outweigh the others—as when a soldier falls on a hand grenade to save his buddies, a monk takes a vow of celibacy, or a political prisoner resists torture.

What is the nature of these social motives? Where do they come from? Are they inherited biological motives or do they arise through a child's learning experiences while growing up in the society of other human beings? At an earlier time they were thought to be innate, instinctive motives. Darwin, for example, said that ". . . the social instincts lead an animal to take pleasure in the society of its fellows, to feel a certain amount of sympathy with them, and to perform various services for them." In man, this basic social instinct leads to the development of civilized society and a sense of social ethics. William James listed sociability, sympathy, love, jealousy, and imitation as basic social instincts. William McDougall, you will recall, included a gregarious instinct in his list. In all these theories, man's tendency to group together, form affectionate ties, and be influenced by social approval or disapproval is attributed to an unlearned biological urge.

Although the idea of a basic social motive seems to make sense intuitively, the instinct theorists began to elaborate upon this idea, postulating an ever-increasing number of social instincts—usually without much real evidence. For every bit of complex social behavior, a special social instinct was involved. For example, some insisted that there was an inborn instinct for modesty. This assertion made a great deal of sense to these Victorian gentlemen, but anthropologists kept reporting on tribes where no one felt the need for clothes. It was quite apparent that the instinct theorists were turning their own learned cultural values into biological imperatives. Anthropological evidence made it obvious that social motives vary so greatly from society to society that to a large extent they must be learned, not inherited.

Thus, psychologists of the twenties and thirties challenged the innate basis of social motivation just as they challenged the innate basis of curiosity and similar motives. Again, most theorists assumed that social motivation is derived from the more basic motives of hunger, sex, and fear. It was held that the attachment of a child for its mother, for example, is learned on the basis of her feeding the child. This kind of social drive is, thus, secondary or derived. In other words, man is a biological creature motivated by visceral tensions and nothing else. However, since he lives in the society of others and depends on them for fulfilling his organic cravings, he develops secondary social needs. In the last chapter, it turned out that the curiosity family of motives was independent of the homeostatic, sexual, and emotional motives. So, too, it is possible that the derived-motivation theorists have gone too far and that there may be an innate basis for, at least, the more undifferentiated social motives.

In this chapter, we shall show how the several theories of derived motivation account for social behavior. Then we shall consider the evidence for the possibility that there are social motives independent of viscerally based drives.

CONCEPTS OF DERIVED SOCIAL MOTIVATION

The three theorists discussed in the last chapter—Freud, Allport and Miller—have extended their analysis of derived motivation to include social motives. The basic concepts—sublimation, functional autonomy, and acquired motivation—have been explained. All three are really quite similar. The extension of each theory will be described briefly in turn.

Freud did not believe that there is an innate social instinct that serves to bring people together. Instead he suggested that people are drawn together by sexual feelings. These feelings may not appear as directly sexual but may be partially inhibited, blunted, and disguised. They appear as ". . . the affectionate relations between parents and children, which were originally fully sexual, feelings of friendship, and the emotional ties in marriage which had their origin in sexual attraction."

According to Freud, a child's attachment to the mother is basically a sexual one. The very young infant, in the oral stage, learns that the mother is the source of oral pleasure. The child is made anxious by the threat of losing the mother because he has learned that she is necessary for the gratification of his instincts. Later on, during the phallic stage, the boy's attachment for the mother is sexual in a genital sense. Because of castration anxiety, however, the sexual attraction must be eliminated. What happens to the sexual motivation here? Freud suggests that part of the sexual energy is used for the process of identification with the father and part of it is sublimated into tender, desexualized feelings for the mother.

In this manner, Freud explains the comradeship between a father and son and the affection between a mother and son as derived from sexual motives. So, too, a little girl's emotional attachment to her parents, as well as her desire for children, are explained as sexual derivatives. Freud goes further. The ties between members of a group are derived from the sexual feelings in the family situation. The bond between a leader and a follower is based on the father-son relationship while the attachment of group members to one another represents sibling relationships.

The most important theoretical question about the concept of the transformation of instincts is whether the basic social attachment between child and mother—from which all the other social relations and interests spring—represents a sublimated sexual motive. That is, are feelings like love, affection, dependence, tenderness, and attachment sublimated forms of sexual motivation? Many of the early followers of Freud broke away from him on this very point. They felt he was wrong in deriving all human warmth and feeling from sexual motivation. Alfred Adler proposed that man is motivated more by social urges than sexual motives. Man, he claimed, has an inborn social interest and desire to relate himself to other people. This process begins in the infant-mother relationship and later is extended to social relations, group identification, and empathy for other human beings. Erich Fromm postulated a basic motive for relatedness, Karen Horney spoke of the need of the child for security in relation to his parents, and Harry S. Sullivan emphasized human relationships. The significant thing about these views is that they have been made by psychoanalytic theorists who dealt with patients in psychotherapy as Freud did. However, they differ from Freud in seeing some sort of basic social motive that is independent of sexual and aggressive impulses.

Our second theorist, Allport, believes that gregariousness is acquired. The demand of the infant for the physical comfort of the mother eventually leads to a desire for the "social, aesthetic, and mental" companionship he later evidences. In answering critics of this conception—which in essence denies an innate social motive—Allport insists that this is "about as simple and straightforward a statement of empirical fact as we are likely to find in the realm of motivation." * Therefore, it is quite clear that affection, sociability, and the other social motivations are, for Allport, transformations of physiological motives like hunger and pain.

Similarly, Allport doubts the existence of a "parental instinct." Many mothers, he says, are not eager to have children and may even hate their offspring when they arrive. The mother may perform her duties only to avoid the criticisms of neighbors or for fear of the law. These extrinsic motives hold the mother to her job, however, until, through practice, child care becomes a joy. Her love for her child develops and the earlier extrinsic motives are forgotten.

Again Bertocci takes issue with Allport. He assumes that there are several basic social motives. He does not accept Allport's assumption that the love of the child for its mother grows out of her physical care but rather believes it has an innate basis. So, too, he believes that there is a parental instinct. These innate social motives may be stultified by the experience of a particular person. Thus, the cases Allport mentions of women who hate their children may involve a background of rejection. Bertocci mentions the case of a woman whose own mother and father had been brutal to her. She grew up not wanting

* G. Allport. Motivation in personality: reply to Peter A. Bertocci. *Psychol. Rev.,* 1940, 47, 533–534.

children or even marriage because she was afraid she would mistreat her own child. She had the desire to be tender to her offspring but was too emotionally blocked to express it. In the case of the basic motive of love, Bertocci suggests that the initial love towards the mother is later expressed toward wife, children, or friends. The motive was an innate social one to begin with but the means of expressing it changed with the development of the person.

Finally, how does Miller dispose of social motives? With John Dollard, he gives examples of how social motives are learned on the basis of acquired drives and rewards. For instance, the attachment of a child for its mother is based, they hold, on the fact that she feeds him, keeps him warm, removes painful stimuli, and tends to his other primary drives. Dollard and Miller point out that during the first year of life the mother is associated with feeding on several thousand occasions. Thus, the mother becomes an acquired reward, and affection for her is derived from hunger, pain, and other primary drives.

In addition to affection, Dollard and Miller explain the social motives for gregariousness, sociability, dependence, approval, conformity, imitation, pride, and honesty as learned. The strength of each acquired motive depends on the specific conditions of learning, which may vary with the family, social class, or society. Thus, Dollard and Miller can account for the great variability in social motives. For example, fighting is valued in lower-class children but disapproved in those from the middle class. In our society competitiveness is a prevalent and approved form of behavior but it is frowned upon in other cultures.

We have already seen that the evidence for acquired drives based on hunger is weak. Therefore, it is rather difficult to see how all these social motives could be derived in this way. Miller, himself, has proposed a new theory of *drive channeling* to replace the acquired-drive notion in the case of positive motives like hunger. We shall discuss this new idea later.

EVIDENCE FOR INNATE SOCIAL MOTIVES

It is easy to observe in man and many other animals the kind of attachment between the young and the mother that we have been discussing. The gosling follows the goose, the young monkey clings to the belly of its mother, and the human infant nuzzles the breast. It is also easy to see the strength of the attachment of the young for the maternal object—separation produces frantic fear. It is considerably more difficult to decide whether the motivation for this attachment is hunger or affection. In fact, it is possible to do so on the basis of naturalistic observation alone. We must turn, therefore, to an experimental method of separating out the two effects.

This is precisely what was done in an extremely important experiment by Harry F. Harlow and his associates. As part of their general experimental work with monkeys, they decided to raise some infant monkeys without monkey mothers, feeding them by bottle and housing them alone in individual cages. To make life a little easier for the infant monkeys they covered the hard floor with a folded gauze diaper. It was then that they made the interesting observation that the infant monkeys became attached to these

Figure 11. An infant monkey in a cage with both wire and cloth surrogate mothers. Although fed on the wire mother, the infant prefers to cling to the cloth mother. (Courtesy H. F. Harlow, Primate Laboratory, University of Wisconsin. Photographs by Robert Sponholz.)

cloth pads—they clung to them and became angry if they were removed. The behavior is remarkably similar to that of a young child with his "peace and security" blanket or the teddy bear he must take to bed with him. It seemed that there was some direct need for "contact comfort" which had little to do with feeding.

In order to test this observation experimentally, Harlow and his co-workers constructed the two "surrogate mothers" shown in Figure 11. One consisted of a cylinder of wire mesh with an opening for a baby-bottle in the center of the "breast"—this was called the "wire mother." The other—the "cloth mother"—was a similarly shaped block of wood covered with cotton terry cloth. A baby-bottle could also be inserted through her "breast." Both surrogates were decorated with lovely monkey faces that had nothing to do with the experiment.

In the main experiment, newly born monkeys were placed in a cage containing one wire mother and one cloth mother. For half the group, the feeding by baby-bottle was done through the wire mother, for the other half through the cloth mother. The question was whether the infant monkey would form an attachment on the basis of feeding or of contact comfort. According to the Freudian theory, the attachment should be based on the oral gratification associated with feeding. According to the theories of functional autonomy and acquired drives, the attachment should be based on the hunger-reduction associated with feeding. In other words, all theories of derived social motives would predict that the attachment should be based on the nursing experience.

The results were just the opposite. The infant monkeys that were fed on the cloth mother spent nearly all their time clinging to "her" and practically none at all on the wire mother. Of course, this would be expected by the theories of derived motivation. However, those monkeys fed on the wire mother also spent most of their time on the cloth mother. They would climb up the wire mother to eat but then scamper back to the cloth mother. The attachment to the cloth mother occurs a little faster when the feeding is associated with her but the attachment of the wire-mother-fed monkeys to the cloth mother is just as strong after a few weeks. Possibly nursing directs the response to the contact comfort of the cloth mother a little more quickly, but it is the contact comfort itself that forms the basic attachment to the surrogate mother. Thus, these studies support the idea of an innate social motive rather than the theories of derived social motives.

Can this simple clinging response be called "love" or "affection"? One thing we usually mean by a baby's love for its mother is the feeling of security and protection it gets from her. This feeling was demonstrated with the infant monkeys by exposing them to fearful stimuli—a strange open room, which baby monkeys find frightening, or a diabolical spider monster. In these situations the baby monkeys would run to the cloth mother in panic, cling to her, and then visibly relax. Secure again, they would cautiously begin to explore the strange place, returning to the home base of the cloth mother from time to time. Who has not seen this in a human child brought into a strange house? But this security-producing contact was not provided, in the monkey studies, by the wire mother—even if the monkey had been fed on her. Again, it is the contact comfort of the soft round cloth figure, not the stimulus associated with feeding, that provides the security.

Can this attachment to a cloth mother be established at any time in the development of the young monkey? The answer appears to be no. If the monkey has an opportunity to cling to the cloth mother during a critical period from about 30 to 90 days of age, the attachment is strong and the security deep. But if a baby monkey is raised in total isolation for, say, six months and then given a cloth mother, only a partial attachment is formed, one which easily crumples when the monkeys are fearful. These monkeys who have missed the critical period of attachment often show "autistic" behavior when placed in a strange and frightening situation. That is, they crouch and rock monotonously instead of going to the cloth mother for security.

These effects continue to operate for years and influence the whole emotional development of the monkeys. Monkeys raised with wire mothers or in plain wire cages show an absence of affection, a lack of cooperation, exaggerated aggression, and a total lack of sexual responsiveness in relation to normally reared monkeys. Those raised with cloth mothers show less aggression and some sexual responsiveness but of an immature kind. It is clear that, although cloth surrogate mothers are superior to wire ones, emotional development is enhanced far more with a real, live monkey mother.

In a recent series of studies, Harlow and his associates have found that to a very large extent experience with other young infants may make up for the lack of a real mother. Infants raised on cloth surrogates were permitted daily interactions with a dozen others in a gymnasium-like playroom. They demonstrated normal play and sexual development, and affectional bonds formed between them. It might even be possible for a member of another species—a human being for example—to provide some part of the maternal stimulation needed for normal affectional development.

What applicability do these animal studies have for human behavior? Actually, there is a remarkable correspondence between many of Harlow's findings and studies of human children who have been deprived of normal mothering. Years ago, Margaret Ribble reported on some 600 children who either had no mother, had inadequate mothers, or had lost their mothers. Such children became negativistic, depressed, and physically weakened. Some of them developed a condition known as *marasmus*, in which they simply wasted away and died.

Similar findings have been reported in a number of studies of children placed in orphanages or foundling homes. In most of these places the food and medical care is adequate, but the shortage of personnel means that the children get no attention except for feeding and diaper changing. Many of them simply lie in their cribs with little physical or emotional stimulation. Those infants who have had no mothering during the first year of life appear to withdraw and are devoid of emotional feelings. Many of them have permanently lost the capacity to form a human attachment. Children who have had some mothering during the first year and are then separated show more dramatic emotional changes. When initially separated from their mothers, these children become anxious and cry, but eventually this reaction changes to depression and apathy. The babies lose weight and show intellectual and language retardation. They stare at nothing, show autistic symptoms such as incessant rocking, and cannot bear to be picked up by anyone. They seem to have lost a basic social responsiveness and to have become emotionless automatons. Sometimes intensive psychotherapy with a warm, loving person can bring them out of their withdrawal.

Older children who have been brought up in this impersonal kind of institution have a disturbed and unsocial kind of personality. They have little control over aggressive impulses, and exhibit various forms of immature, delinquent, and antisocial behavior. They do not form close emotional ties, remaining withdrawn and unattached. In other words, children who do not receive affection during the early critical years do not develop a basic social motive for love and affection.

Writing from a modern psychoanalytic point of view, John Bowlby concludes from these studies on maternal separation that a child's attachment to the mother is primary and not derived from any other motive. Components of this attachment are the instinctive tendencies to suckle, cry for the mother, cling to her, follow her, and stay close to her. Separating the child from the mother produces what Bowlby calls "primary anxiety." This anxiety is not based on fear of losing a person the child has learned protects and feeds him; rather it comes before such experiences and represents an innate need for social attachment.

There is still a great deal that is not known about the development of affectional bonds. Stimulation during an early critical period appears to be essential, but some controversy persists over the exact nature of the required stimulation. Some people have simply written it off as tactile, but this explanation seems oversimplified. There may be species differences. For instance, the imprinting phenomenon in the duck, which we mentioned in Chapter 1, seems to be an analogous form of primary social tie. Yet this involves visual contact and following rather than tactile stimulation. In Harlow's recent studies, infant monkeys prefer a rounded form permitting clinging or a rocking mother-surrogate to a flat, cloth covered, nonmoving board. On the human level, vocalization may be at least as important as cuddling.

Now we turn to the other side of the primary social relationship between child and parent—particularly the mother. There is no doubt that the maternal motive is a powerful one—mothers of many species fight for and die for their offspring. Nevertheless, this powerful motive serves no homeostatic purpose for the mother and may operate against her personal survival. Naturally, it serves the important biological function of species survival, but it operates as a social motive—that is, it is aroused in the mother by another organism.

Is it not possible that the maternal motive is simply the outgrowth of a hormonally based urge to nurse? This would be analogous to the theories of the affection of the child for the mother based on nursing—one biological organism on each end of the breast, so to speak. Nursing is important but not the whole story.

In higher animals, the mother's early *emotional* experiences seem to be crucial in controlling her maternal behavior. Several of the monkeys raised without a real mother in the Harlow studies have become mothers themselves. Now, ordinarily a normal monkey mother handles, clasps, and nurses an infant soon after birth. It is very difficult to take the infant from the mother at that time—Harlow reports that a team of men is necessary to get the infant away. In contrast to this strong maternal behavior, motherless monkey mothers show an almost complete lack of interest in their offspring, ignoring them, rebuffing their attempts to make contact, and even attacking them. Harlow reports that most of these infants would not have survived without hand-feeding by the human caretakers.

It should be noted that these inadequate mothers were hormonally normal and capable of nursing. Furthermore, all the stimulus elements were there—it was even noted that the infants made desperate attempts to make contact with the mothers even when they beat them off repeatedly. The critical factor, then, was the social experience of the mother herself during her first year or so of life. The degree of social experience seems important here. Infant monkeys raised on surrogate mothers but allowed contact with other infant monkeys or human beings showed adequate maternal behavior. Similarly, the experience with the first infant may arouse some affectional motivation in the mother although it is not immediately apparent. Two of these inadequate mothers have now had a second infant and show maternal behavior. In fact, the maternal behavior seems exaggerated, with the mothers overprotecting the infants and not allowing them to break physical contact until much later than normal monkey mothers do.

A woman's maternal feelings are also dependent on her emotional experiences as a child. Clinical observations on the human level support Harlow's findings that mothers who are emotionally deprived themselves frequently have difficulty in relating to their children. Similarly, overprotective mothers may be seeking affection from their children and thus prevent their developing independence.

Development of Social Motives

Even if we accept the idea of a basic, innate social motive that is developed during a critical early experience of an affectionate relationship, we are still a long way from explaining complex social motives. It is possible that many general social motives—gregariousness, friendship, group membership—are simply extensions of the basic tie with the mother. As we have seen, something along these lines seems to be important in the development of the parental motive. Nevertheless, the early ties remain the strongest and the generalization of affectionate ties is not indiscriminate. We feel closest to family members, a little closer to our own subcultural group than to others, and closer to our own countrymen than to others. Unfortunately, only a few unusual people really feel a close bond with all humanity and all human suffering.

Three mechanisms have been proposed to account for the development of social motives, and they are basically the same. The first is Freud's concept of *cathexis*. Within his theory of sexual libido, he assumed that a certain amount of libidinal energy would be attached (cathected) to any object gratifying the infant. Initially this would be the mother's breast and finally the mother as a whole person. This association could then be extended to other people capable of gratifying the child's sexual motives. The second mechanism is Neal E. Miller's new theory of the *learned channeling* of motives, developed to supplement the acquired-motivation theory mentioned earlier. Miller points out that all people have an undifferentiated hunger motive at birth but later on develop specific tastes and aversions due to social learning. Thus, one may learn to enjoy eating snails. However, this taste is not an acquired motive removed from the hunger motive, since the snails do provide for a reduction of the hunger drive. Miller doubts that a taste could be acquired for sawdust. Thus, hunger is continuously involved. Another motive is not grafted on to it; rather, the hunger motive is directed into certain channels. The third concept, *canalization*, is almost identical to cathexis. Gardner Murphy has emphasized this concept, although he credits the French psychiatrist Pierre Janet with the term, and points out that the idea is really very old. Murphy gives examples of acquired food tastes as does Miller but also adds instances of the development of aesthetic tastes.

If we accept the evidence in the previous section suggesting an innate social motive, the concepts of cathexis, channeling, and canalization may provide an excellent explanation of the development of love, affection, and social feeling. A child is born with a nonspecific motive for certain sensory-emotional experiences that can only be provided in full by a social relationship with another person. For a baby monkey, even another baby monkey provides more of these experiences than a carefully constructed mother surrogate. Without the necessary sensory-emotional experience during the early critical period, the basic social motive may never be canalized outward. No one knows whether it simply disappears or is turned inward, producing the withdrawn and autistic child. Ordinarily the mother provides these sensory-emotional experiences, so the primary social motive is canalized to her. As the child grows, more and more of these sensory-emotional experiences canalize the social motive towards her and we say that an affectional bond has been established between the child and mother.

The establishment of wider affectional bonds—with the father, the play-mates, and the social group as a whole—can be achieved as additional sensory-emotional experiences with other people add new canalizations of the social motive. However, the new canalizations must be based on satisfaction of the basic social motive—it is not merely a generalization of affection from the mother to others. If the father, for instance, is unloving, even to the point of rejecting the child, no affectional bond would be expected to develop.

The social development of the child would be strongly influenced by the specific canalizations of the basic social motive. For example, recent studies by Albert Bandura indicate that a child tends to *identify with,* or model his behavior after, those people who have shown him affection. Thus, a little boy with a cold, rejecting father may have difficulty in imitating masculine traits. On the other hand, if a strong affectional bond is developed between the father and son, the father may use the threat of loss of affection, or even mild disapproval, to direct the son's behavior. Thus, a father may mold the son's interests, hobbies, athletic participation, occupational choice, selection of friends, and many other aspects of social behavior.

Later on, the canalizations are broadened so that the school child is influenced by values of his playmates, the college student by the expectations of his fraternity brothers, and the adult by his membership in a particular social class, ethnic group, political party, religious organization, professional association, or social community. Sociologists and anthropologists have studied these value systems in different groups and cultures so that we know something about what behavior is expected. But in order to know more about how an individual will actually behave in a given situation, we must know the history of the canalizations of the basic social motive.

SOCIAL MOTIVATION AND THE SELF

The picture is still incomplete. The child is influenced by the parents' expectations even when they are not immediately present to approve or disapprove. Adults may continue certain behavior long after the parents have died. Not even the most loyal organization man is buffeted about entirely by the shifting demands of the people around him. Social motives are more personal; they *feel* as if they come from within, some sort of internalization has taken place. The motives are usually in reference to the person himself: "*I* want the approval of my group," "It is *my* need to achieve," or "*I* would feel like a heel if *I* did this or that."

In trying to make the concept of functional autonomy work, Allport finally came to the conclusion that only those activities that had become "personalized" or "ego-involved" would tend to persist. Numerous experiments have shown that human subjects will perform better on a task if they are "ego-involved" in it. For example, if the instructions are simply that the experimenters are trying out some new tests, the subjects tend to be sluggish. But if the instructions are that the task measures intelligence, personality, maturity, or somthing else important to the subject, they typically perk up. They have become "ego-involved" because the task has some personal relevance.

Several terms have been introduced to account for this internal factor which seems so important in social motivation. The term *ego* is common, but I prefer the term *self* because it is more widely used by psychologists and social scientists with different theoretical orientations. Not all psychologists, however, would agree that a term like *self* is necessary. In fact, some would reject the concept because a *self* can never be directly observed, only inferred. Still, I think that the concept of the self, or something like it, is critical in understanding social motivation.

Psychoanalytic theorists, especially, have emphasized that at first an infant probably cannot distinguish between himself and the rest of the world, between his body and that of his mother, between fantasy and reality. Slowly a concept is built up, partly through the interaction with the physical environment but most importantly through social interaction. Harry S. Sullivan, a cultural psychoanalytic theorist, suggests that the self is built up out of the reflected appraisals of significant people in the social environment. When the mother is warm and loving the child thinks of himself positively (the Good Me in Sullivan's terms), but when she is cross or rejecting the child feels anxious and thinks of himself negatively (the Bad Me). This suggests that the self-concept is very largely based on the basic social motive for affection which we have discussed.

We hear appraisals of one sort or another all our lives. "Johnny is naughty," "That's a good boy," "He's smart," and so on. Sometimes they are not heard but felt, as when the mother says nothing but is disgusted with the child's smearing food or playing with his genitals. The love of the mother, and others, is so important to the child that he not only learns what to do or not do to win her approval and avoid her disapproval, but also fashions his concept of what he is and what he ought to be on the same basis. At first he is, say, obedient because it pleases his mother; later, part of his self-concept is that he is an obedient person. Being disobedient raises fears in the child that he will lose his mother's love. Later on, even after the person is far away from his mother, being disobedient may raise anxiety because it is not consistent with the conception of the self as obedient. Thus, the person's evaluation of himself, or his self-esteem, originates in his early affectional relationships and later becomes a powerful motivating force.

People vary drastically in their self-esteem. Some people grow up seeing themselves as basically good and worthy of respect while others see themselves as inadequate. Most people tend to try to keep their self-esteem at the highest possible level. We avoid people who "threaten" us, that is, those who tend to lower our self-esteem. We may remember flattering comments on a term paper more easily than negative ones. Ernest R. Hilgard has interpreted many of the famous Freudian defense mechanisms as ways of maintaining self-esteem through self-deception. For example, we may *rationalize* aggressive behavior by saying that we are protesting social injustice.

The importance of self-esteem has also been demonstrated experimentally. For example, in one experiment "level of aspiration" was studied in well-adjusted and poorly adjusted adolescents. The task was a simple one of matching shorthand symbols to letters of the alphabet. At the end of each trial they were asked to estimate how well they thought they would do on the next trial—the estimate being their "level of aspiration." In general, subjects in this sort of situation tend to set their goals for the next trial a little higher than the score they just received. Most of the well-adjusted students did so. The poorly adjusted adolescents, however, showed two deviant kinds of goal setting—either they lowered their estimate of success on the next trial or they set unrealistically high goals. In other words, the fear of failure was so great that they lowered their level of aspiration so that they could be sure of success or else they *compensated* for their feelings of inadequacy by setting goals they had little hope of attaining. These poorly adjusted adolescents appeared to be desperately trying to maintain a shaky self-esteem.

Therefore, we see that the desire to maintain or establish a positive evaluation of the self operates as a powerful motive. It is intertwined with many of the social motives we shall discuss later. It helps explain why some people will endure physical hardships, hunger, and pain because of pride in self. It is important to remember that the self-concept grows out of the important family relationships in childhood and in all probability is primarily influenced by the basic motivation for social relationships we have discussed. Thus, to threaten a man's self-esteem is to threaten his expectations that he is a worthwhile person, capable of being loved, cared for at a time of need, and holding a position of some security and dignity in the society of his fellow men.

Social Motives
in Action

Although the origins of social motivation are still shrouded by the mists of incomplete evidence and theoretical controversy, there is little disagreement on the importance of social motives in human behavior. Whether they be innate, learned, or both, social motives dominate most of our everyday behavior. In this chapter, we shall be concerned primarily with social motives as they influence behavior. Although we shall examine the social conditions under which these motives develop, we shall not be concerned with the question of their innate or derived origins.

First of all, what social motives are there? Numerous

8

lists have been proposed and others could be constructed. One of the most influential is Henry A. Murray's list of "psychogenic needs." The psychogenic needs, or social motives in our terms, were not arrived at capriciously. A small number of normal subjects were studied most intensively with interviews, questionnaires, and specially designed psychological tests. One of these, the Thematic Apperception Test, is now widely used as a personality test. The TAT consists of a series of pictures of people in various situations. The subject is asked to use his imagination and write a story about each picture. Social motives can be inferred from the imaginative stories and checked by other evidence. On the basis of this sort of intensive analysis of living and breathing human beings, Murray presented a tentative list of 20 social motives. These are shown in Table 1 along with brief definitions.

TABLE 1

List of Murray's Social Motives

Social Motive	Brief Definition
Abasement	To submit passively to external force. To accept injury, blame, criticism, punishment. To surrender. To become resigned to fate. To admit inferiority, error, wrongdoing, or defeat. To confess and atone. To blame, belittle, or mutilate the self. To seek and enjoy pain, punishment, illness, and misfortune.
Achievement	To accomplish something difficult. To master, manipulate, or organize physical objects, human beings, or ideas. To do this as rapidly and as independently as possible. To overcome obstacles and attain a high standard. To excel oneself. To rival and surpass others. To increase self-regard by the successful exercise of talent.
Affiliation	To draw near and enjoyably co-operate or reciprocate with an allied other (an other who resembles the subject or who likes the subject). To please and win affection of a cathected object. To adhere and remain loyal to a friend.
Aggression	To overcome opposition forcefully. To fight. To revenge an injury. To attack, injure, or kill another. To oppose forcefully or punish another.
Autonomy	To get free, shake off restraint, break out of confinement. To resist coercion and restriction. To avoid or quit activities prescribed by domineering authorities. To be independent and free to act according to impulse. To be unattached, irresponsible. To defy convention.
Counteraction	To master or make up for a failure by restriving. To obliterate a humiliation by resumed action. To overcome weaknesses, to repress fear. To efface a dishonor by action. To search for obstacles and difficulties to overcome. To maintain self-respect and pride on a high level.
Defendance	To defend the self against assault, criticism, and blame. To conceal or justify a misdeed, failure, or humiliation. To vindicate the ego.
Deference	To admire and support a superior. To praise, honor, or eulogize. To yield eagerly to the influence of an allied other. To emulate an exemplar. To conform to custom.

TABLE 1 (Continued)

List of Murray's Social Motives

Social Motive	Brief Definition
Dominance	To control one's human environment. To influence or direct the behavior of others by suggestion, seduction, persuasion, or command. To dissuade, restrain, or prohibit.
Exhibition	To make an impression. To be seen and heard. To excite, amaze, fascinate, entertain, shock, intrigue, amuse, or entice others.
Harmavoidance	To avoid pain, physical injury, illness, and death. To escape from a dangerous situation. To take precautionary measures.
Infavoidance	To avoid humiliation. To quit embarrassing situations or to avoid conditions which may lead to belittlement, the scorn, derision, or indifference of others. To refrain from action because of the fear of failure.
Nurturance	To give sympathy and gratify the needs of a helpless object: an infant or any object that is weak, disabled, tired, inexperienced, infirm, defeated, humiliated, lonely, dejected, sick, mentally confused. To assist an object in danger. To feed, help, support, console, protect, comfort, nurse, heal.
Order	To put things in order. To achieve cleanliness, arrangement, organization, balance, neatness, tidiness, and precision.
Play	To act for "fun" without further purpose. To like to laugh and make jokes. To seek enjoyable relaxation from stress. To participate in games, sports, dancing, drinking parties, cards.
Rejection	To separate onself from a negatively cathected object. To exclude, abandon, expel, or remain indifferent to an inferior object. To snub or jilt an object.
Sentience	To seek and enjoy sensuous impressions.
Sex	To form and further an erotic relationship. To have sexual intercourse.
Succorance	To have one's needs gratified by the sympathetic aid of an allied object. To be nursed, supported, sustained, surrounded, protected, loved, advised, guided, indulged, forgiven, consoled. To remain close to a devoted protector. To always have a supporter.
Understanding	To ask or answer general questions. To be interested in theory. To speculate, formulate, analyze, and generalize.

From C. S. Hall and G. Lindzey. *Theories of personality.* New York: Wiley, 1957.

If you examine Murray's list carefully and apply it to your friends and yourself, you will find it a remarkably sensitive description of the motivational patterns in everyday life. The next time you are having a post-mortem after a difficult examination, keep your eyes open. You may notice that some people attack the professor for giving an unfair examination (Aggression). Others take their grade as an indication of their own inadequacy (Abasement). Others simply resolve to work harder (Counteraction). Some may not admit their grade or may even lie about it (Defendance). A few might drop the course (Infavoidance). In this sort of situation, some people may give a few words of sympathy and encouragement (Nurturance) to those who seem to want it badly (Succorance). Other examples will come to mind.

It would be possible at this point to discuss each of the social motives a little bit. However, this would do justice to none of them. Therefore, we shall select two for more extended discussion. These two—achievement and affiliation—have not only been studied in more detail than the others but are also of considerable interest in themselves. Nevertheless, while this chapter will seem heavily weighted in favor of achievement and affiliation motivation, you should keep in mind that they are simply serving as representatives of at least a score of social motives. At some future time these other motives will be fully enough explored for similar presentations.

ACHIEVEMENT MOTIVATION

The achievement motive has been most extensively studied by David C. McClelland and his associates. The method of investigating achievement motivation is an extension of Murray's TAT approach. Typically, subjects are presented with four TAT cards flashed on a screen and are then asked to write a five-minute story guided by several questions. The pictures are either selected or specially constructed to suggest achievement themes. Afterwards, the stories are scored for achievement content.

Achievement was defined by McClelland as performing in terms of a standard of excellent or, simply, as a desire to be successful. In scoring for achievement motivation each story is read and a general decision made about the presence or absence of achievement imagery. If achievement imagery is present, the scorer then makes judgments about the occurrence of specific components of achievement, such as the expression of a desire for achievement (for instance, "He wants to be a doctor"), the description of activity instrumental for success ("He will try his best"), or the anticipation of reaching his goal ("He is thinking of the day when he'll be famous"). These and other components are given scores and then added up to provide a numerical index of the strength of the achievement motive in a given individual. The measure is somewhat complex but, with sufficient practice, two undergraduates can reach satisfactory agreement on the scoring.

Here is an example of a story showing a strong achievement theme. It was written in response to a picture showing a young boy in the foreground and a hazy operation scene in the background:

This young boy is dreaming of the day he will have completed his training and become a great and famous doctor. Perhaps this portrays someone already famous for research. He has been asked by his father or relative what he wants to do when he grows up and he is trying to tell them the mental picture that he has in his mind of himself in thirty years. The boy is thinking of the great thrill that must be experienced by a doctor when he performs a delicate operation saving someone's life. The boy will go on through college and eventually become a world-famous doctor.*

It is quite clear that this subject expresses a strong desire to be famous and successful. The subject might deny such strong achievement motivation if asked about it point-blank, but is able to reveal it in this fantasy situation. His ambition may not necessarily be in the direction of medicine, but might be in the areas of business, literature, or social work. The medical content of the story is dictated by the picture, but other subjects concentrate on the fear of an operation or guilt feelings about someone's having been hurt.

Does the achievement motive facilitate learning and performance? Recall that this is one of the key definitions of a motive. Actually, quite a few studies have demonstrated that individuals with a high achievement motive will learn and perform responses faster and better than those with a low achievement motive. It should not be concluded, however, that individuals with high achievement motivation will automatically do better on any and all tasks. They may not excel on boring and routine tasks where there is no challenge. It is necessary that their sense of achievement be engaged. This need is shown quite clearly in a study by Elizabeth G. French. She had Air Force cadets do a simple coding task under three different conditions: In the relaxed condition subjects were told in a casual way that the experimenter was just trying out some tests; in the task-motivated condition other cadets were told that the test measured intelligence and that the results would influence their career; the third group was extrinsically motivated with a reward for the five best scorers of leaving the testing situation an hour early. Achievement motivation was also measured by a verbal form of the McClelland test and each group was divided into high- and low-achievement people.

The results of French's experiment show that under the relaxed conditions there was no appreciable difference between the high- and low-achievement subjects—the high achievers were not challenged. Under the task-orientation conditions, however, when the questions of intelligence and career were raised, the high achievers did get involved and performed better. Perhaps the most interesting finding turned up under the extrinsic reward conditions. The low-achievement subjects did respond a bit to the lure of an hour's free time but the high achievers did not very much. Other studies support this finding— high achievers are not easily motivated by extrinsic prizes and so forth. They do best when they get some achievement satisfaction from doing a task well in relation to some standard of excellence.

What are these high-achieving people like in other ways? They tend to have self-confidence, to like individual responsibility, and to prefer concrete knowledge of the results of their work. They get good grades. They are active in college and community activities, choose experts rather than friends as working partners, and are resistant to outside social pressure. They enjoy taking moderate risks in situations that depend on their own ability, but not when it comes to pure chance situations, such as horserace betting.

In general, high-achieving individuals seem to have many of the characteristics of the hard-headed, ambitious business man. It is not surprising that

* From J. W. Atkinson (ed.) *Motives in fantasy, action, and society.* Princeton, N. J.: Van Nostrand, 1958.

they prefer occupations like stock broker or factory manager. This relationship led McClelland to believe that entrepreneurs—the organizers, risk-takers, and economic builders of the world—are primarily motivated by the desire for achievement.

Now, McClelland's theory runs counter to the assumption made by most economists, as well as the man in the street, that entrepreneurs are driven by the "profit motive." McClelland points out, however, that greed for money is not limited to entrepreneurs. For example, the money lenders of India are surely as profit-minded as the nineteenth century British capitalists but without the "empire-building" qualities. The entrepreneur ploughs his money back into business expansion. Furthermore, McClelland finds the same sort of entrepreneurial behavior in factory managers in communist countries where the profit motive would be at least minimized. Yet these communist managers strive for expansion, productivity, and success.

According to McClelland, entrepreneurs are primarily driven by the achievement motive. They are interested in profits and personal income because it serves as a measure of their competence. Thus, the money becomes a symbol of success. McClelland presents evidence that managers in countries as diverse as the United States, Italy and communist Poland have high achievement scores. The high-achievement people just want recognition in the concrete form of money for their efforts at achievement.

How does a person come to develop a motive for achievement? It seems to depend on the values of his parents and the emphasis they place on this sort of thing. For example, Marion Winterbottom measured the achievement motivation of a group of eight-year-old boys in a small Midwestern community and related it to their mothers' descriptions of their child-rearing practices. She found that the mothers of boys with high achievement motivation made demands for independence and mastery at an earlier age than did the mothers of the boys with low motivation for achievement. For instance, by the time the highly motivated boys had reached age seven, their mothers had begun demanding that they know their way around the city, that they try new and difficult things on their own, that they be active and energetic, that they make their own friends, and that they do well in competition. These mothers made relatively few restrictions on the behavior of the boys, but those they did make, they expected to be mastered at an early age. These mothers also evaluated their boys' accomplishments quite favorably and rewarded them with hugs and kisses. The mothers of the low-motivation group, on the other hand, were more restrictive and did not encourage self-reliance, so that the boys remained more dependent on the family.

AFFILIATION MOTIVATION

Another important social motive is affiliation. The affiliation motive is quite different from the achievement motive and to some extent diametrically opposed to it. A person motivated mainly by achievement may make important contributions to society, but he may not be the most comfortable person with whom to live. Other people are more concerned with human relationships. Recall that achievement-motivated individuals prefer to work with experts in order to get a task finished. Those with a strong affiliation motive prefer to work with friends or congenial companions even if the task suffers somewhat. Obviously, there is a basic difference here about what things are most important.

The definition of affiliation motivation by Murray is given in Table 1. Essentially, it refers to a desire to be with people in an affectionate and friendly relationship. For purposes of scoring TAT stories, the affiliation motive has been defined as a "concern in one or more of the characters ever establishing, maintaining, or restoring a positive affective relationship with another person. This relationship is most adequately described by the word friendship." A scoring system analogous to that used for achievement motivation has been devised for affiliation. This includes expressing a desire for a friendly relationship, a fear of rejection, activities towards establishing a relationship, and the attainment of a close relationship as a goal. Certain TAT pictures are better for getting affiliation stories than others. Here is an example of a TAT story showing a lot of material suggesting affiliation motivation:

Two college buddies who haven't seen one another for a long time. A chance meeting and they are glad to see one another. It is probably a class reunion or frat founders day. They were very close friends in college. They are probably reminiscing. They will have an evening together and make arrangements for future meetings.*

The TAT measure of affiliation has been shown to be effective in several situations. For example, T. E. Shipley and J. Veroff administered a *sociometric questionnaire* to the members of a fraternity. In this procedure, each fraternity member was asked to rate the personality of each of his brothers in terms of aggressiveness, friendliness, conceit, timidity, cooperation, and so on. The questionnaire was administered in the fraternity house with each member standing up in turn to be rated by the rest of the group. It was thought that this situation would arouse a fear of possible rejection and a motive for affiliation. Immediately after this, the TAT was administered and scored for affiliation motivation. In comparison to another, similar fraternity, not given the sociometric questionnaire, the experimental group wrote stories with much more affiliation content.

How does the affiliation motive affect performance? The individualistic, achievement-motivated individual works hard when he gets involved in a problem. The person motivated primarily by affiliation, however, may not be so involved in getting the job done. People mean more to him than the task. In fact, this sort of person may find it difficult to stay in his room alone to study—he would much rather be at a bull session or out on a date. Are there any situations in which the affiliation motive facilitates task performance?

Elizabeth French did a study in which she compared the task performance of achievement- and affiliation-motivated individuals under two different conditions. The task was for a group of four people to reconstruct a short story from 20 sentences or phrases. Each member of the group had five of the items on cards and could tell the others about them but not show them the cards.

* From Atkinson. *Ibid.*

Half the groups consisted of people with high achievement motivation and half of people with high affiliation motivation.

The two experimental conditions consisted of different *feedback* information. What this means is that each group was stopped several times during the task and told how well they were doing. Half of the achievement and half of the affiliation groups were told that they were working efficiently. Specific things they were doing well were mentioned, such as reading off all cards immediately, identifying characters, and roughing out possible plots. Notice that this information is all couched in terms of getting the task done. This was called *task feedback*. On the other hand, the remaining achievement and affiliation groups were given *feeling feedback*. This information was all put in terms of the social harmony of the group. They were told that the group worked well together, and then they were praised for giving everyone a chance to contribute, not becoming impatient with poor suggestions, keeping arguments friendly, and so on. It is quite clear that the two kinds of feedback had quite different appeals.

The groups were scored in terms of the number of phrases correctly inserted, with a bonus for finishing within the time limit. The results showed that the achievement-motivated groups did best with task feedback. The affiliation-motivated groups did not do so well with task feedback but they did do quite well with feeling feedback. Apparently, information specifically tied to the task is helpful or even motivating to achievement-oriented subjects but not to affiliation ones. However, affiliation-motivated subjects respond well to information about the more human aspects of the situation whereas the achieving ones do not. French also reports that the general atmosphere in the two types of groups was markedly different. The achievement groups were eager to complete the task and argued violently. The affiliation groups were quieter and less intense, showing more friendly interest in one another and the experimenter.

The next question is how the motive for affiliation develops. Is there anything comparable to the independence training given the achievement-motivated children? Unfortunately, we know much less about the development of affiliation. Some general observations suggest that the parents of affiliation-motivated children put more emphasis on close family ties and conformity to parental authority. They seem to encourage dependence rather then independence. However, these facts have not yet been established on a firm basis.

There is some evidence that affiliation is related to anxiety. Using a measure of affiliation different from the TAT, Stanley Schachter demonstrated that increasing anxiety tended to increase motivation for affiliation. Groups of coeds were asked to participate in an experiment and then told that they would be subject to rather painful electric shocks. They were shown some diabolical electrical apparatus; then they were told there would be a ten-minute delay before the experiment began. During this time, they could wait alone or with the group. This was the high-anxiety condition. In the low-anxiety condition, no apparatus was shown and subjects were reassured that the shock would be mild and painless. Actually, no one in either group was ever shocked. The whole point was to see whether they wanted to be together or alone when frightened.

The results showed that most of the women in the high-anxiety group wanted to wait with the others while most of those in the low-anxiety group did not care one way or the other. In other words, anxiety increased affiliation. Waiting together seems to reduce anxiety for some people. The exact reason why has been a matter of considerable research interest. Some evidence suggests that anxious individuals want to compare themselves to others so as to evaluate their own emotions and decide just how frightened they should be. However, this comparison would have to be done on a nonverbal basis, because anxious people want to wait together even when they are not allowed to talk. Other investigators suggest that waiting together provides an opportunity for catharsis or distraction. Finally, it may be that some people simply have learned to seek out others when anxious—like Harlow's monkeys clinging to the cloth mother.

Along these lines, Schachter made another interesting discovery. It was primarily those coeds who were the first ones born in a family or who were only children that wanted to affiliate when anxious. Later-born children had less of this tendency. In fact, third-borns had less of this tendency than second-borns and fourth-borns less than third-borns. Schachter's finding suggests that earlier-born children have a greater opportunity to learn to be dependent on their parents.

The situation is not quite that simple, of course. For one thing, men and women differ in dependence according to some studies. In our culture, it is less acceptable for a male to be dependent and to seek the comfort of others. Then, too, the type of anxiety seems to be important. In one study with male subjects, fear of electric shock increased affiliation, but anxiety about having to suck baby bottles seemed to make the subjects want to wait alone. Perhaps the latter experiment aroused too much anxiety about dependence. In any case, there are a number of factors involved. Nevertheless, the theme running through all this research is that the affiliation motive involves training in dependence during childhood, whereas the achievement motive involves independence training.

SOCIAL MOTIVES AND SOCIETY

Social motives like achievement and affiliation, as we have seen, have important influences on performance under various conditions. We have also seen that these social motives are quite strongly influenced by child-rearing methods, parental values, and family structure. The question that now arises is, how are these social motives in the individual related to the society as a whole? There is obviously a relationship between the motives of the individual members of a society and the dominant values of that society. It is also quite possible that there is a relationship between these individual motives and social values, on the one hand, and the economic growth, political structure, and cultural level of the society on the other.

Most historians, economists, and sociologists explain individual motives in terms of the conditions in the society in which a man lives. Thus, for example, David Riesman suggests that as medieval European civilization began to give way to the rise of capitalism, society needed entrepreneurs to develop industry and cope with an expanding population. Other people point to the discovery of natural resources, the presence of an ideal climate, or the opening of a new marketing area. The great historian Arnold J. Toynbee simply says that if the environmental and social stimulus is just right—not too easy and not too hard—a society makes a creative response.

David C. McClelland finds fault with all these views. He does not deny that these factors are important. For example, tropical climates may provide a lush food supply so that there is little motivation for change, while severely cold climates may require all of a person's energies just to maintain life. So, too, under some circumstances, a population increase may stimulate the economy. It is also true that the discovery of oil in an impoverished desert land has a profound effect on the economy. McClelland made systematic studies of a large group of countries falling in the temperate zone, where climatic factors should be minimized. He found that an expanding population was not always associated with prosperity—it frequently produced a decline in economic growth. He also found that countries equated in terms of economic resources differed greatly in the exploitation of these resources. Something else must be involved.

McClelland proposes that the something else is psychological—the social motivation of the people in a country. Specifically, he suggests that those countries that developed a strong motive for achievement in their children reaped economic gains in the years to come as the children developed into entrepreneurs. Furthermore, McClelland devised an ingenious test for this hypothesis.

First of all, McClelland had to find a measure of economic growth that would be comparable for the 40 temperate-zone countries he studied. This is not a simple matter, but he finally decided on amount of electrical power produced by a country relative to its population. All industry depends on electrical power, so it provides an index of economic development. Power figures were available for 1929 and 1950. The several countries differed greatly in the increase in electrical power production during this period.

For the measure of achievement motivation, McClelland wanted something that indicated the degree of stress on achievement to which the children were subjected. He selected children's reading books at the second-, third-, and fourth-grade levels in general use around 1925 and 1950. Stories were selected at random from these readers and scored for achievement motivation with a system similar to that used for TAT fantasies. Now he had a measure of achievement emphasis just before the period of economic growth or decline and another at the end of the period.

The results showed that there was a positive relationship between the degree of achievement motivation in children's readers around 1925 and the economic growth in terms of electrical power production changes from 1929 to 1950. That is, those countries which showed the greatest gain in electrical output (such as Great Britain) had high stress on achievement in the 1925 children's readers, but those with a small gain or a loss (such as Belgium) laid little stress on achievement. On the other hand, there was no relationship between the achievement shown in the 1950 readers and the gain in electric power output. This last point is important. It means that the achievement themes in the children's readers are not the *result* of economic expansion. Instead, it seems that an important factor in economic growth is the motivation emphasized to the children of the previous generation. The implication is that if the children get motivated to achievement, they will do the things needed to expand the economy when they grow up. Motivation precedes economic development!

Is it possible that the rise and decline of the great civilizations of the past depended on achievement motivation? McClelland tested this idea, too. Take the classical Greek civilization centered in Athens, for example. Ancient Greece began developing economically during the eighth and seventh centuries, B.C., but it was not until the sixth century B.C. that Athens began to show what kind of a civilization it was going to become. During the fifth century B.C. it reached its climax in the Golden Age of Pericles. This was the period when the familiar figures of Aeschylus, Sophocles, Euripides, Aristophanes, Socrates, Plato, and Aristotle lived and made their tremendous contribution to Western civilization. This was also a period of great economic strength. Shortly after this, Athens lost the Peloponnesian War to Sparta and began to decline.

Now, the traditional view is that the rise of this glorious civilization was caused by economic expansion. This expansion in turn produced the achievement-oriented person associated with a growing civilization. The decline is usually attributed to the unsuccessful Peloponnesian War, which was thought to drain off the energies of the Athenians and cause a loss of motivation. McClelland, however, takes the position that the motivation for achievement preceded the period of maximum growth and that the decline of the civilization was preceded by a decline in achievement motivation.

How to measure economic growth and achievement motivation in such an ancient civilization? McClelland and his associates decided to use the area of trade as an index of economic development, because much of Athenian prosperity was based on foreign trade reaching from the Atlantic to the Black Sea. The extent of this trade area at different times could be assessed by the places at which Athenian jars have been unearthed. These carried the wine and olive oil that formed the bulk of the trade. The jars of the sixth, fifth, and fourth centuries can be dated by style and design, while the places in which they have been found have been recorded. Thus, it is possible to draw a rough map of the area of trade for the three centuries that correspond to the periods of growth, climax, and decline of Athenian civilization.

Achievement motivation in Athenian civilization was measured from samples of literature—dramas, funeral orations, poems, war speeches, and so on. An equal number of each type was selected from the period of early growth (900 to 475 B.C.), the climax (475 to 362 B.C.), and the decline (362 to 100 B.C.). Homer is an example from the period of early growth, Pericles from the climax, and Demosthenes from the decline.

The results are shown in Figure 12. It can be seen that the trade area of Athens rose from about 1.2 million square miles in the sixth century B.C. to 3.4 million square miles in the fifth, and then declined to 1.9 in the fourth century. This shift illustrates the economic expansion and decline and also parallels the cultural flowering and fading. The measure of achievement motivation shows an interesting thing. Achievement—the striving for success —was highest in the early period of growth; it preceded the economic and cultural climax. At the time of the climax it had actually fallen and continued

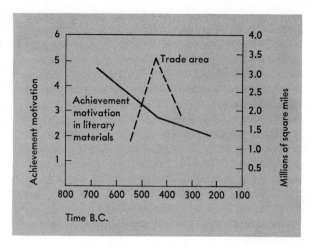

Figure 12. Achievement motivation and the rise and decline of Athenian civilization. The fortunes of Athenian civilization are shown by the extent of the area of trade. Achievement motivation —as shown in literary materials—was high before the peak of the civilization and began to decrease before the decline. (After D. C. McClelland. The achieving society. Princeton: Van Nostrand, 1961.)

to fall during the decline. This finding puts an entirely new light on the Peloponnesian War. The spirit of Athens was not destroyed by the war, it was already decaying. Much has been written about the personal degeneracy of Athenians during their golden period. It is likely that this loss of motivation is what lost the war.

The question still remains: What factors determine an increase in achievement motivation in a society? We have seen that achievement motivation is fostered in a child by things like parental warmth, nondominant father, and high achievement standards. However, the question can be pushed further back: Why do the parents behave in just this way? One possibility is that parents are unaware of the long-term effects of their child-rearing methods. In other words, the parents want independence in their children and incidentally produce high achievers. On the other hand, parents who push their children too much towards achievement may find that the children reject achievement altogether. This explanation, in a sense, attributes achievement to accidental or fortuitous circumstances.

The religious and ethical beliefs of a culture may influence social motivation. The German sociologist Max Weber attributed the rise of capitalism in Northern Europe and North America to what he called the "Protestant Ethic." In contrast to the worldly renunciation, brotherly love, and disavowal of usury in the traditional Catholic faith, the Protestant Ethic teaches that personal success and the accumulation of capital is good in the eyes of God. Hard work is the best defense against religious doubts, feelings of unworthiness, or sexual desires. McClelland has gone on to test this hypothesis. He found that electric power production rates, relative to natural resources, were higher in Protestant than Catholic countries. It would seem that entrepreneurial behavior is fostered more by the religious ideas of Protestantism than Catholicism.

The key religious ideas associated with achievement and economic growth are not the usual doctrinal differences between Protestantism and Catholicism. Instead there are certain "core values" that can be found running through many of the world religions which are relevant here. In India, for example, it is the ascetic Jain and Parsee sect members who are conspicuously successful in business rather than the Hindu Brahmans. Zen Buddhism is associated with economic success in Japan. Jewish business advance has been linked to the rise of the antirabbinical Hassidic movement. As McClelland characterizes them, the core values in these achieving sects include an emphasis on individual rather than ritualistic religious experience, a stress on self-reliance rather than a dependence on religious experts, and very frequently some sort of asceticism or self-denying attitude. In short, the Puritans of the world!

Let us stop for a moment and consider the implications of these theories and facts. It is really quite amazing that a psychological variable like achievement motivation is so important in economic matters. We do not mean to discount the role of traditional economic factors, but, as McClelland points out, he was able to tell more about economic growth from children's readers than from population data. It is even more amazing that human ideas should be so relevant. Now, it is understandable that a university professor is so impressed by the importance of ideas, but perhaps many of us have failed to appreciate that man its not necessarily a passive victim of his history and his environment; he is capable of conceiving great plans and molding the world to them.

Epilogue

We have come a long way —from the acquisition of stinging cells by the Microstoma to the rise and fall of Athenian civilization. The rubric of Motivation and Emotion covers an immensely diverse and complex area. We have seen something of the ebb and flow of attempts to grasp conceptually this difficult set of phenomena—instincts, drives, intrinsic motives; one-motive, three-motive, and multi-motive theories; homeostasis, brain functioning, and biological effectance; learned motives, unlearned motives, and many-faceted motives; and physiological and social determinants. We have the exciting new discoveries—pleasure and pain centers in the brain; motives for curiosity, exploration, and play; and the primacy of love, affection, and contact-comfort. What are the implications of all of this? Where is the psychology of motivation leading?

It is my contention that the field of motivation and emotion is in a period of creative flux that is gradually leading to a new image of the nature of man. In the past, the field of motivation and emotion was dominated by two theories—the classical Freudian and the classical behaviorist. The Freudian image of man was that of a creature driven by inherited, unconscious sexual and destructive instincts constantly seeking release in a frustrating social environment. The behaviorist view was that of a creature quietly metabolizing in the shade, occasionally goaded into action by the hot sun and the lure of a cold glass of beer. There is probably not a psychologist alive who would accept either of these views today, but what is the new image like?

To begin with, the old battle between heredity and environment is largely dead. Man is not thrust into the world with ready-made, inflexible instincts nor is he a passive piece of clay that society models into neat value systems. Man is born with a great many potentialities that interact with a complex physical and social world to form a spectrum of motivational systems. There is probably not a single motive that is entirely innate or entirely learned. Biological potentialities are channeled and inhibited, expanded and contracted. We still do not know what man's full potential is.

There is increasing agreement that man's potential depends largely on his incredibly intricate brain. Motivation is not a simple matter of visceral tensions and tissue needs. Motivation depends on a brain that contains mechanisms for pleasure and pain, that controls its own level of arousal, and that is sensitive to external as well as internal events. Probably all motives contain internal and external features.

Man is not simply warding off noxious stimuli and seeking the peace of death or nirvana. He actively interacts with the environment. He is curious, playful, and creative. He conceives great ideas, seeks meaning, and envisions new social goals—these products of his own imagination influence his own striving, his own motivational pattern, and the course of civilization.

Finally, human warmth and relatedness are not epiphenomena grafted on to a peristaltic rhythm. Giving and receiving love are every bit as much a part of human biological nature as the need to urinate. We lust but we also seek affection. We hate but we also seek closeness and esteem. We even try to love and esteem ourselves.

This image of man is emergent, but perhaps man himself is emerging. We are well aware that many men do not fit this image. The brutal psychopath who throws a bomb into a Sunday school classroom seems consumed by hate—and maybe fear. The hungry people of the world could not care less about creativity and sometimes not even about the love of their close ones. Some motives may have to be fulfilled before others emerge. It is possible that there is some sort of a hierarchy of motives.

Abraham Maslow has suggested that man has a number of primary, instinctive motives ranging from *lower* motives to *higher* ones. These are arranged in a hierarchy that corresponds to the assumed evolutionary level of the motive. First come the *physiological motives* like hunger, then the *safety motives* like fear, then the *love motives*, the *esteem motives,* and finally, the motive for *self-actualization*. The lower the motive, the more crucial it is for survival and the earlier it appeared in evolution. The hierarchy also refers to the order of appearance of motives in the development of the individual—the physiological motives appear early, the esteem ones later, and self-actualization much later, if at all.

Now we come to Maslow's most important point—a higher motive does not usually appear until the ones below it are satisfied. Hungry Koreans risk their lives to pick up scrap on an American Army firing range; only well-fed people can indulge in the luxury of being safe and secure. As strong as the love motives are, a fearful person may shy away from others. As fear is reduced, the love motives emerge. When the love motives are satisfied, the esteem motives appear. A person who needs love desperately may sacrifice his self-respect, crawl back to a tormenting love object. Obviously, there are many exceptions to this hierarchy—the mother who dashes into the burning house to save her children, the captured native who is too proud to eat the taboo food, and so on—but the idea is quite suggestive.

Finally, when all lower motives are satisfied, Maslow says, a motive for *self-actualization* emerges. This is a difficult concept to describe because so little is known about it. Maslow means the desire for self-fulfillment, to do what one is fitted for, to actualize what one is potentially. For one person it may mean being an ideal mother, for another a first-class athlete, for still another a creative artist. Maslow has made clinical studies of people he considered to be self-actualizing—fully functioning college students and historical figures like Abraham Lincoln, Albert Einstein, Eleanor Roosevelt, and Jane Addams. He found that these people are realistic, accept themselves and others, are spontaneous, autonomous, and creative, and are able to enter into mature love relationships.

Still, so little is known about the self-actualizing motive that it must be considered as an hypothesis. It does point up, however, the fact that the study of human motivation is nowhere near complete. Perhaps the future will bring research into man's self-actualizing tendency, into the motivation for man's philosophical, religious, and ethical strivings, into man's search for the meaning of his existence. These are the distant frontiers of a rapidly developing field; we do not have the answers. Perhaps you, the reader, will provide some of them at some time in the future.

Selected Readings

Chapters 1 and 2

Carroll, J. B. *Language and thought.* Englewood Cliffs, N. J.: Prentice-Hall, 1964.

Hochberg, J. E. *Perception.* Englewood Cliffs, N. J.: Prentice-Hall, 1964.

Hyman, R. *The nature of psychological inquiry.* Englewood Cliffs, N. J.: Prentice-Hall, 1964.

Lazarus, R. S. *Personality and adjustment.* Englewood Cliffs, N. J.: Prentice-Hall, 1963.

Mednick, S. A. *Learning.* Englewood Cliffs, N. J.: Prentice-Hall, 1964.

Chapter 3

Bindra, D. *Motivation—a systematic reinterpretation.* New York: Ronald, 1959.

Brown, J. S. *The motivation of behavior.* New York: McGraw-Hill, 1961.

Hall, J. F. *The psychology of motivation.* Philadelphia: Lippincott, 1961.

Murray, E. J. *Sleep and motivation.* New York: Appleton-Century-Crofts, 1964.

Teitelbaum, P. *Physiological psychology.* Englewood Cliffs, N. J.: Prentice-Hall, 1965.

Young, P. T. *Motivation and emotion.* New York: Wiley, 1961.

Chapter 4

Ford, C. S., and F. H. Beach. *Patterns of sexual behavior.* New York: Hoeber, 1952.

Kinsey, A. C., W. B. Pomeroy, and C. E. Martin. *Sexual behavior in the human male.* Philadelphia: Saunders, 1948.

Kinsey, A. C., W. B. Pomeroy, C. E. Martin, and P. H. Gebhard. *Sexual behavior in the human female.* Philadelphia: Saunders, 1953.

Lazarus, R. S. *Adjustment and personality*. New York: McGraw-Hill, 1961.

Monroe, R. L. *Schools of psychoanalytic thought*. New York: Holt, Rinehart and Winston (Dryden), 1955.

Chapter 5

Arnold, M. *Emotion and personality*. Vol. I. *Psychological aspects*. Vol. II. *Neurological and psychological aspects*. New York: Columbia University Press, 1960.

Rethling Shafer, D. *Motivation as related to personality*. New York: McGraw-Hill, 1963.

Rotter, J. B. *Clinical psychology*. Englewood Cliffs, N. J.: Prentice-Hall, 1964.

Young, P. T. *Motivation and emotion*. New York: Wiley, 1961.

Chapter 6

Berlyne, D. E. *Conflict, arousal, and curiosity*. New York: McGraw-Hill, 1960.

Fiske, D. W., and S. R. Maddi (eds.). *Functions of varied experience*. Homewood, Ill.: Dorsey, 1961.

Woodworth, R. S. *Dynamics of behavior*. New York: Holt, Rinehart and Winston, 1958.

Chapters 7 and 8

Atkinson, J. W. (ed.). *Motives in fantasy, action, and society*. Princeton, N. J.: Van Nostrand, 1958.

Lambert, W. W., and W. E. Lambert. *Social psychology*. Englewood Cliffs, N. J.: Prentice-Hall, 1964.

McClelland, D. C., J. W. Atkinson, R. A. Clark, and E. L. Lowell. *The achievement motive*. New York: Appleton-Century-Crofts, 1953.

McClelland, D. C. (ed.). *Studies in motivation*. New York: Appleton-Century-Crofts, 1955.

McClelland, D. C. *The achieving society*. Princeton, N. J.: Van Nostrand, 1961.

Mussen, P. H. *The psychological development of the child*. Englewood Cliffs, N. J.: Prentice-Hall, 1963.

Schachter, S. *The psychology of affiliation*. Stanford, Calif.: Stanford University Press, 1959.

Schein, E. H. *Organizational psychology*. Englewood Cliffs, N. J.: Prentice-Hall, 1965.

Stacey, C. L., and M. F. DeMartino. *Understanding human motivation*. Cleveland: Allen, 1958.

Epilogue

Maslow, A. H. *Motivation and personality*. New York: Harper, 1954.

Index

Physiological need:
Miller's definition, 33
and psychological drive, 26–27
and rewards, 30–32
Piaget, J., 77
Plato, 3
Play instinct, 70
Pleasantness-unpleasantness dimension, 57–58, 62
Pleasure center, in brain, 31–32
Plutchik, R., 56–57
Problem-solving, and motivation, 16–17
Psychogenic needs, 97
Psychological drive, and physiological need, 26–27
Psychological motive, Miller's definition, 33
Psychosexual stages, Freudian, 43–47
Punishing area, in brain, 31

R

Raymond, S., 54
Recovery, of stimulus, 77
Reflexes, 5
Religious values, and motivation, 107–108
Repression, of memory, 15–16, 66
Reticular activating system, 61–62, 82
Reward:
acquired, 73
and brain stimulation, 31–32
defined, 8
and hunger, 29–30
incentive value, 13
and learning, 12–13
and need-reduction, 30–32
Ribble, M., 90
Richter, C., 26
Riesman, D., 104
Roberts, W. W., 31, 61
Roussel, J., 66

S

Saccharine, and hunger-reduction, 31
Sarason, S., 63
Satiation mechanism, 29
Schachter, S., 50, 103–104
Schlosberg, H., 59
Schwartz, M., 41
Scott, J. P., 25
Self:
aggression against, 67
and social motivation, 93–95
Self-actualization motive, 111
Self-concept, 94–95
Selye, H., 60
Sensory deprivation studies, 75–76
Sensory motives, intrinsic, 75–76
Sensory receptors, and sexual behavior, 37
Set, and perception, 14
Sex, as motive, 39–41:
deprivation and satiation effects, 40–41
in learning, 39–40
Sex hormones, 35–37
Sexual behavior, physiology of, 35–39
Sexual development, 42–47:
Freud's psychosexual stages, 43–45
maturation, 42–43
psychosexual stages and culture, 45–47
Sexual motivation, and guilt, 19

Sexual reward, 40
Sherif, C., 55
Sherif, M., 55
Shipley, T. E., 102
Social behavior, and hunger, 18
Social learning, and sexual behavior, 38–39
Social motives:
derived motives, 85–87
development, 92–93
innate motives, 87–92
and instinct theories, 84
Murray's list (*table*), 97–98
and the self, 93–95
and society, 104–108
Sociometric questionnaire, 102
Speisman, J. C., 54
Spinal reflexes, and sexual behavior, 37
Spinoza, B., 3
Stimulus, and drive, 28
Stomach contractions, and hunger, 24
Stomach stimulation, and hunger-reduction, 29–31
Stress, reaction to, 60–61
Sublimation, 71
Sullivan, H. S., 86, 94
Sympathetic nervous system, 60

T

Taste receptors, and hunger-reduction, 29–31
Test anxiety, 63
Thalamus, and emotions, 50, 61
Thematic Apperception Test, 97, 99–100, 102
Thinking, and motivation, 16–18
Thirst:
and homeostasis, 22–23
and perception, 14
Thirst-reduction, 30
Threat, appraisal of, 54–55
Tinbergen, N., 6
Toynbee, A. J., 105

U

Unconscious motives, 19–20

V

Veroff, J., 102
Visceral responses, in emotion, 49–51, 62
Vogel, W., 54

W

Washburn, A. L., 24
Watson, J., 6, 51, 53, 56
Weber, M., 107
White, R., 81
Will, 3
Winterbottom, M., 101
"Wisdom of the body," 25–26
Wolfe, J. B., 73
Woodworth, R. S., 6, 81

Y

Yerkes-Dodson Law, 12–13, 17, 64
Young, P. T., 4, 33, 63

Z

Zeller, A. F., 15